#NobodyToldMe

The truth about Down syndrome

This book is made possible due to the generous contributions of parents of children and young people with Down syndrome–who have both shared their personal experiences to enlighten and educate, and generously donated towards its design, production and distribution.

ISBN: 978-1-909929-35-7

First published in June 2020 by

#NobodyToldMe that the scenic route could be so beautiful!
#TheyToldMe we would struggle

#NobodyToldMe your eyes would sparkle like diamonds
#TheyToldMe you would look different

#NobodyToldMe that you would make an impact on everyone
you meet in the most amazing way!
#TheyToldMe you would struggle to communicate

#NobodyToldMe that your determination to achieve anything
you put your mind to would inspire me every day
#TheyToldMe that milestones would be delayed

#NobodyToldMe you would have the biggest heart and the purest soul
#TheyToldMe you might not understand emotions

#NobodyToldMe you would be the best brother to your sisters
#TheyToldMe you would be a burden to your siblings

#NobodyToldMe that you would be the best thing to come into our family
and that you would teach us all more than we could ever teach you

Written by Cheryl McCauley of Charlie

Contents

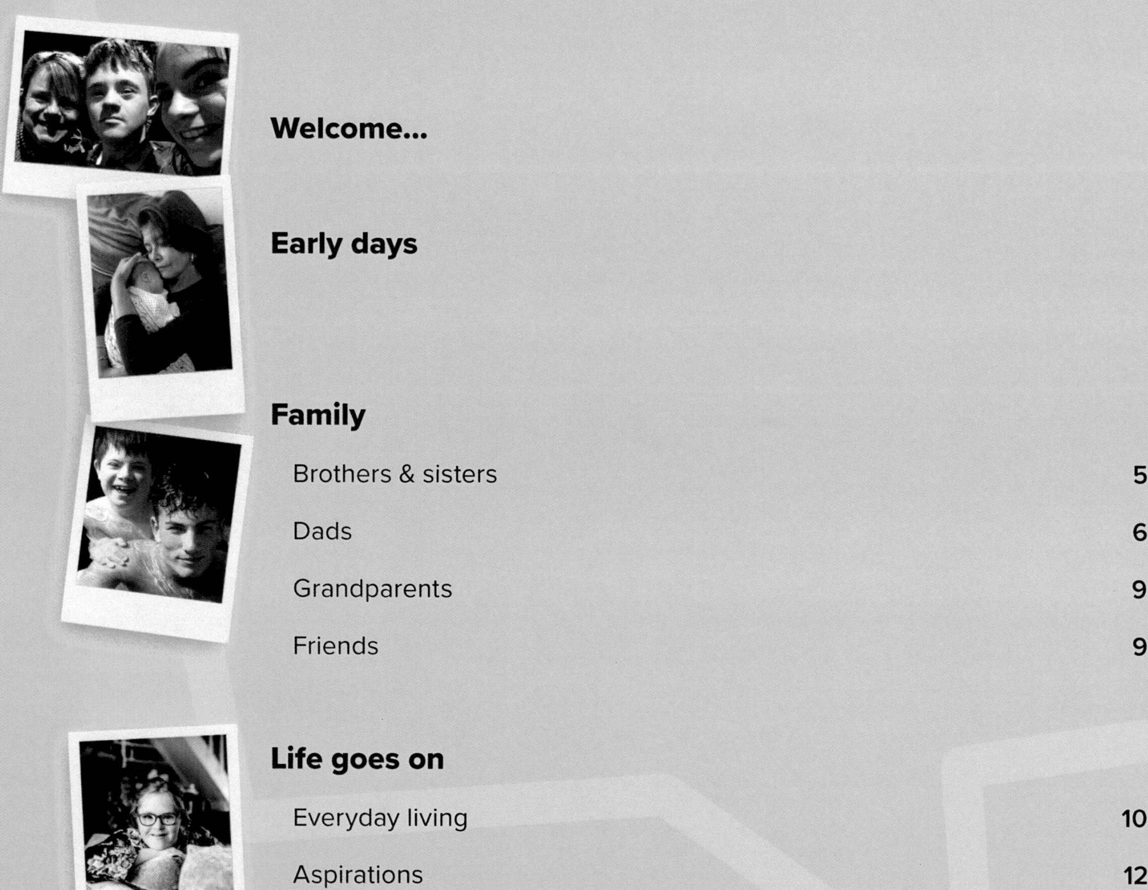

MOET & CHANDON
GAP
MET

Welcome...

Growing up, all I had ever wanted, apart from to be Agnetha from Abba, was to get married and have children. Life strangely rarely goes to plan; the closest I got to achieving my Agnetha aspiration was driving to Ikea in a Volvo listening to Abba, and having kids turned out to be equally challenging. I suffered four miscarriages before our beautiful daughter Emily was born. Keen to have another child, at 39 I knew the chance of having a baby with Down syndrome was high; after private tests and concerns at my 20 week scan, I found myself booked in for an amnio. I knew we would consider termination – society and medics expected that course of action. I also knew an amnio carries a risk of miscarriage and so cancelled it, which is probably the best decision I have ever made.

When Tom was a day old, the paediatrician asked me if I thought my precious baby looked 'normal'. My world fell apart. It took me a year to fall back in love with Tom and realise that there was never anything wrong with him, but rather, everything wrong with my and society's attitudes and perceptions – including my own.

All parents respond to their child's needs and parents of a child with Down syndrome are no different. Our children with Down syndrome often teach us to re-evaluate and appreciate what is important in life – to love and to be loved.

Tom will never achieve the exam results his sister Emily attained, but I don't love him any less. Emily will never have the same level of emotional empathy that Tom has, but I don't love her any less. Both my children have endearing qualities, both have flipping annoying traits, both make my heart burst with pride and both give me sleepless nights (which – in my book – is what parenting is all about).

#NobodyToldMe that Tom would make my heart burst with love and pride nearly every day, or that he and Emily would be the loves of my life and I will always love them no matter what...

Nicola Enoch, mum to Tom

#NobodyToldMe that I'd love you so much I couldn't breathe.

#NobodyToldMe that the pain and grief would turn into pure pride and love.

#NobodyToldMe me having a child with Down syndrome wouldn't break me but would actually make me.

#NobodyToldMe that my heart would become so full of love for you.

#NobodyToldMe I would be the envy of all my friends with a baby that slept 12 hours from day one!

#NobodyToldMe how funny your little personality would be.

#NobodyToldMe that you would sing, play music and dance every day before breakfast.

#NobodyToldMe that your love could heal old wounds.

#NobodyToldMe that I needed you, that my life would be happier because you are here.

#NobodyToldMe that when my GP said she was sorry you have Down syndrome, that I didn't have to believe her – that she was wrong.

#NobodyToldMe you would embody empathy and compassion.

#NobodyToldMe that you'd be the best brother.

#NobodyToldMe you would become the strongest link in the family.

#NobodyToldMe that the words Down syndrome that had initially frightened me to the core would eventually be something I would completely accept and embrace because it is a part of you.

#NobodyToldMe that we would make so many amazing new friends along this journey.

#NobodyToldMe that you would look like my other children. I'm ashamed to say I was so scared of how you would look.

#NobodyToldMe how proud and in awe of you I would be.

#NobodyToldMe how much laughter you would bring into our lives, and that your pure unadulterated enjoyment of life would be infectious!

#NobodyToldMe that the real problem was never Down syndrome but rather my own ignorance, others' preconceptions and society's failings.

#NobodyToldMe how you would be able to walk into a waiting room and have everyone smiling and chatting in minutes.

#NobodyToldMe how I wouldn't change you for the world but would try to change the world for you.

#NobodyToldMe that instead of worrying about your future I would be so excited to see the little boy you will become.

#NobodyToldMe you would be one of the best things that could happen to me.

#NobodyToldMe that you would be a magnet for good people and be the light around which our family revolves.

#NobodyToldMe that you'd steal my bed just as much as my heart.

#NobodyToldMe how beautiful you would be.

#NobodyToldMe you would make my heart burst with pride almost every day.

#NobodyToldMe that I would melt into a million pieces at the sound of your hearty laugh.

#NobodyToldMe I could love so fiercely and protectively – or that I could learn to read a complicated, challenging, beautiful, wordless boy whose big blue eyes reflect his love for us.

#NobodyToldMe that you would be such great company with a quick wit and a laugh that lifts my heart.

#NobodyToldMe that it's only bloody Down syndrome!

Early days

Discovering your little one has Down syndrome can be overwhelming and worrying. All too often we are presented with potential health concerns our little one may have now or in the future, and sometimes medical professionals advise what our little one will or won't be able to do.

But the truth is that no one can predict the future for any baby, and every parent I know with a child or young person with Down syndrome has been amazed at just what they can do!

EARLY DAYS

Product review

When I placed my order, I said, “Regular amount of chromosomes, please!” That’s what everyone else got and what I wanted too. They called me shortly after my order was in production and said, “Great news, we went ahead and upgraded you to extra chromosomes for free! You’ll receive the extra chromosomes with your completed order in nine months.” What? I was mad! All the other orders I had seen displayed via perfect Instagram posts did not have an extra chromosome.

Well, I decided that receiving my order with an extra chromosome was better than not receiving an order at all, so I settled in to wait for this surprise upgrade to arrive. I have now had my order for two months and am writing this review to let others know that the upgrade to extra chromosomes is amazing! If offered, definitely take it! I posted a photo opposite of the finished product and you can see that the extra chromosome is so worth it – it is extra cute, extra special, and extra-ordinary! So much extra joy. Would purchase again for sure.

Jessica Young Egan, mum to Gwendolyn

EARLY DAYS

The moment your baby...

... is diagnosed with Down syndrome, the universe injects the most powerful drug known to man straight into your heart. Let's call it 'Enhancenon'.

In small quantities, this drug causes happiness, joy and euphoria – but an overdose of Enhancenon of this magnitude has some profound side effects on 98 percent of the population. Side effects that might be experienced vary vastly in each individual but can include any or all of the following:

Stage 1: Rage, fear and sadness – in any quantity

These emotions are so enhanced, you might feel like you want the world to swallow you up. You might feel you want the world to swallow your baby up, just to make these feelings go away. You might cry uncontrollably or be furious beyond anything you have ever felt before. You might feel grief – this baby is not what you had planned.

Don't fight these feelings – they are all side effects of the overdose. They are not your fault and they certainly are not something you are expected to control at this time.

Stage 2: Heightened awareness

Suddenly every thing is about Down syndrome. Friends especially will relay stories of knowing or having come across a person with Down syndrome. The diagnosis becomes a hot topic. Your eyes and ears pick up and seek out anything linked to the diagnosis. Hawk-like, you will see and hear more than you have ever done before.

Our advice at this time?

FORGET everything you have ever heard before or any assumptions you are making now. Your perception will be skewed because the overdose is still coursing through your veins.

Stage 3: Thinking you are a fortune teller

You will look to an unknown future and think you know what is coming. You will see and plan a future that you think is waiting for you.

Try and ground yourself at this point. Without this diagnosis, you would be marveling at your baby's tiny fingers and tiny toes. You would be happily examining nappy contents and laughing at baby farts. Try and pull yourself back into the here-and-now and do these things.

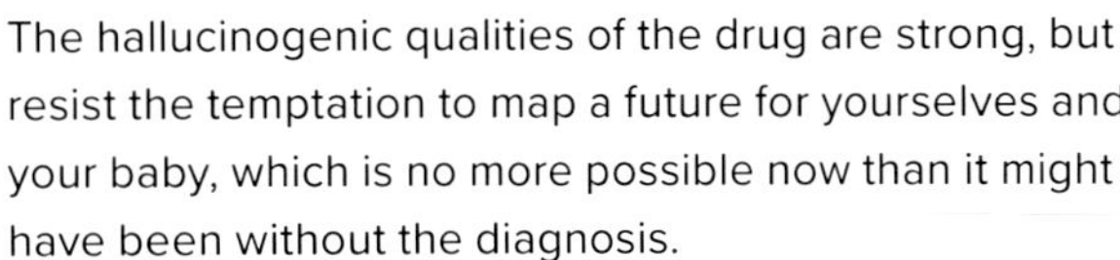

The hallucinogenic qualities of the drug are strong, but resist the temptation to map a future for yourselves and your baby, which is no more possible now than it might have been without the diagnosis.

Stage 4:
The 'fix' stage

You might become obsessed with Googling; obsessed with finding ways to help your baby. Drugs, physio, speech and language, portage, tests, vitamins... STOP! Enjoy your baby. You cannot cure Down syndrome and right now, your baby is a baby and needs you.

Deal with the here-and-now. Deal with any proven medical problems, but the rest should be as it would have been without the diagnosis. Cuddles, cuddles and more cuddles. Let your baby lead the way and it will all fall in to place.

Stage 5:
Opening doors

As your confidence grows, the drug allows you to step outside your comfort zone and make some connections. Slowly, there might be a little prick of realisation coming through the fog: this baby is opening your eyes to something new. It might be frightening, it might be uncomfortable at first, but out there is a whole multinational, multicultural family waiting to embrace you.

Stage 6:
Delirious pride

When you have reached this stage, your body has almost metabolised the drug enough to function normally again. You will see your baby smile or sit up or roll or put food in his or her mouth and your heart will burst with pride. The pride will come from so deep inside that it might make you weep.

The pride will be so much more enhanced than if your child hadn't had the diagnosis. Now the fun bits begin and your eyes will sharpen and you will see your baby! Days will come and go and the diagnosis will not be at the forefront of your mind; your baby will be!

The End

But really, the beginning...

This is the start, the start of your very amazing, wonderful journey together. The day that life overtakes fear, the day that love overtakes presumption. Enjoy it.

Once your body adjusts to the huge levels of Enhancenon, you will look into the eyes of your child and realise that this is the child you always wanted. You will feel much more at peace, much calmer.

The fact of the matter is that, occasionally, Enhancenon will still cause flare-ups of any or all of the original side effects, but for different or altered reasons. As for what Enhancenon is... it is pure, undiluted love.

When you finally adjust to this new life, you will realise how much better it has become – all because of this little, tiny, unexpected diagnosis that means so little in the grand scheme of things. You will end up feeling grateful and realising that you have so much more love in your life now than you ever did before. Thank the Universe.

Helen Kingdon, mum to Seren

EARLY DAYS

We thought the odds of 1/47...

...were quite low but were offered the 'safe test' and decided whatever the outcome we wanted to know and so went ahead. When I got the call to say the result confirmed there was a greater than 95% chance of our baby having Down syndrome I was shocked. I drove home as fast as I could and burst into tears in Tommy's arms.

After an hour or so of feeling sad, I suddenly realized I didn't anymore – it was just the shock, it didn't change anything. Termination didn't need to be discussed, only dismissed as an option. I think for me it was easier to accept quicker than a lot of mums as I had experience supporting young adults with Down syndrome in a previous job. I had a great bond with them so I knew it wasn't something to be sad about. Tommy has a second cousin with Down syndrome so was also unfazed by the diagnosis after the initial shock.

Three months on we have our little girl India Jane and the very idea that we were ever sad about her for even a second now seems ridiculous. She's so utterly gorgeous and smiley and we're already starting to see her cheeky personality come out. The whole family is utterly besotted with her as are we.

Natalie Clinnick, mum to India

EARLY DAYS

It's been nine months...

...since our son Nico was born. You'd think his unexpected arrival at home after 21 minutes of active labour would be my most enduring memory of that day, but it's not. A few hours after he was born, my husband Jordi returned home with the unenviable task of tidying up, and a couple of doctors came to examine Nico. I never imagined that examination would end with the words 'we strongly suspect he has Down syndrome'. It felt as if my world fell apart within those few moments; I couldn't begin to count how many times I used the word 'devastated' during that day, and even that didn't come close to explaining how I felt. I thought I was never going to feel okay ever again.

I was terrified. I didn't want us to be different from everyone else; I didn't want people to feel sorry for us and this child who was 'other'. His life flashed before my eyes. I imagined a forever child-like adult who would always be wholly dependent upon us, and then later a burden to our daughter Alba. I fast-forwarded to him being bullied at school, I mourned that he'd only ever have a 'token' job (if that), would never get married or have children. In those early days when I should have been basking in happiness, I was distraught. I couldn't even say the words 'Down syndrome' without crying.

Close friends and family rallied; with inspirational poems, recommendations of bloggers, texts and visits – all of which helped me feel less alone and suddenly 'different'. They still saw us as the same people, the same family; they celebrated our newborn and made me realise that I should be doing the same. Seeing a dear friend love him as deeply as if he were her own, healed my heart more than she will ever know – and seeing Alba as a proud big sister showed me that if she did not see him as anything other than her brother, then we should not see him as anything but our son. The fear subsided as we came to see Nico as a baby first and his diagnosis second, and started enjoying life with our sweet boy. Nico is a joyful baby; he is quick to smile and loves people. A bundle of energy always on the go, he is inquisitive, cheerful (except when hungry!) and brings us a great deal of happiness.

Like all parents of babies, we have absolutely no idea what his strengths and weaknesses will be, but thanks to therapies and inclusion, children with Down syndrome can be fully incorporated into mainstream schools; learning reading and writing alongside their peers.

As for the future, I am filled with hope that Nico will have a fulfilling, worthwhile, enjoyable life. Not only do people with Down syndrome have 'normal' jobs, but they are now actors (Zack Gottsagen is tipped to receive an Oscar nomination for his role in The Peanut Butter Falcon); models (Madeline Stewart has walked the London, Paris and New York Fashion Weeks, and Kate Grant models for Benefit Cosmetics), town councillors (Ángela Covadonga Bachiller in Valladolid, Stephen Green in Nuthall); and public speakers (John Franklin Stephens). Argentina has just appointed its first pre-school teacher (Noelia Garella) who has Down syndrome, and Bryan Russell is running for Congress in Peru. Given the chance, with help and encouragement, the sky is the limit – people with Down Syndrome can achieve more than was ever thought possible, and have so much to contribute to society. I have read of couples with happy, successful marriages, and there are a huge number of adults living independent lives in their own homes.

So although Nico has an extra copy of chromosome 21 lurking in his genetic makeup, that is only one part of who he is and who he will become – he is first and foremost a person: a son, a brother, a family member, a friend. He will eventually be a classmate, a work colleague, a neighbour – and all we wish is that he be treated with kindness and respect; as an equal human being and as a valuable member of society.

Wendy Sutton, mum to Nico

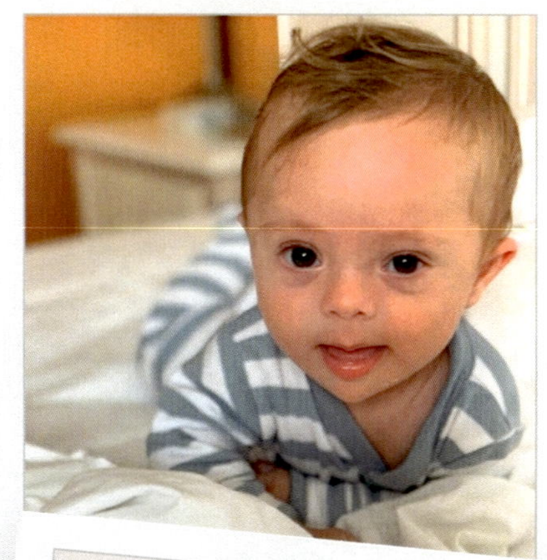

EARLY DAYS

I found out I was pregnant...

...on Christmas eve 2010. I was 16 years old . Young and naive but I soon grew up very fast. The first two scans were amazing – seeing my precious baby on that dark screen, to say I was buzzing about life would have been an understatement. At the 16 weeks scan, the nurse told me I had to come back the next day to the fetal medicine unit. My baby had a large hole in the heart. I was so broken. When I came back the next day, they told me my baby had tricuspid artresia and that he would need major surgery when he was born. I was in deep shock. I didn't know what was happening.

I continued to go for scans every week to see if baby's heart was functioning okay. Weeks passed and then at 27 weeks they ruled out Steven had an AVSD. I was confused and hurt. I really didn't know how to feel.

He was my baby and I was going to do whatever was needed. Doctors advised me to get a termination. I couldn't do it. They gave me half an hour to decide. – I didn't need half an hour, I told them there and then there was no possibility I was going to abort. They told me Steven wouldn't be able to have a good quality of life.

Weeks passed and I went for a 37 week scan. They took me into the family room. The doctors came in with a very worried look, they said "We are sorry but your baby will possibly be born with Down syndrome." I was worried, I was scared, I was sad – all because of the negative way I was addressed by the doctors. They decided to take me in the following week to start my labour and in August 2011 I gave birth to not only my best friend but the most amazing, beautiful, kind-hearted little boy in the whole world. They said "We're sorry but Steven has Down syndrome". I looked down and thought 'okay son let's do this no matter what we will get there together'.

Steven was born with Hirshsprung's disease in the bowel. He has a permanent ileostomy bag. He handles life so well, he's such a strong little boy. Altogether he has had 18 operations including heart surgery – but he doesn't complain, he gets on with his life and I wouldn't be without him.

Nine years later and my sister Chelsea is pregnant. We were at the midwife the other day and Chelsea wanted the screening test as she wanted it to come back high risk! The midwife said "Oh that's great news, you're one in 1500" and we both said "Aw that's crap!" The midwife was confused. I told her that I actually have a son who has Down syndrome – she soon changed her tune!

Danielle Urie, mum to Steven

EARLY DAYS

Dear Doctor

I know it's early in the morning and you have just come on shift. It's a Monday too – the start of another busy week in Paediatrics. And a midwife has come to tell you that you need to see the baby boy in Bay 1.

And you are dreading examining him. Because if the midwife is pretty sure she's seen those signs, then you know she's probably right. But it will be left to you to confirm it and deliver the news to a mother with no idea. Then you walk in the room and see her and your heart sinks a little lower. She's got that new mother glow and happiness about her, and you know you are about to break her world.

But don't be scared.

Don't be scared of all those little signs you are hoping you won't see, but are there. See those eyes? The ones shaped like large almonds with the epicanthal folds? Well soon they will open wide. They will have Brushfield spots (another common trait) that will make them shine like they have had diamonds placed in them. Those eyes will see the world and look deep into the soul of those around him and steal their hearts. See that nose with it's flat nasal bridge? That will be the cutest nose his sister has ever seen. See those feet? The ones with the sandal toe gap? Those feet will soon walk and he will follow his daddy everywhere. He will walk 130 miles around Anglesey with his daddy before he reaches 4. They will kick a ball and they will run. See that floppiness? That's caused by low muscle tone that will become stronger. It will leave those around him in awe of how hard he works to get stronger.

It will also leave him able to give the best cuddles. And those hands? Those hands you are dreading unfolding to see the single line crease? Those hands will build blocks and hold books. Those hands will grasp his mother's hand every night before he sleeps. And she will dread the day he gets too old and stops.

So Doctor, don't be scared. Those things you see aren't there to be feared. They are the very things that make him beautiful and make him powerful. They are the things his family will adore. Yes, you are about to change this mother's world, but you will not break it. You are about to tell her that she's just welcomed something wonderful into her life. Don't tell her you're sorry because you shouldn't be. Tell her congratulations. Tell her that the road ahead may not always be easy. But tell her it will always, always be worth it.

From: The Mum of the baby boy in Bay 1

Maria Belton, mum to Joseph

EARLY DAYS

After a long IVF journey...

...we were blessed with a positive pregnancy test. As two Mummies we were worried about the reaction we would get from people, but those two lines made all the worries disappear and suddenly nothing else mattered.

When we got the call to say we were 'high risk' (one in 89), we didn't think anything could have knocked us further back, until the call after when the NIPT advised we had a greater than 99 per cent chance of our precious baby girl having Down syndrome.

We cried, we hugged, we cried some more, and researched until there was no more research to do. Labour was nowhere near as scary as we had been told and after 19 hours our Elsie arrived.

We held her, we kissed her and we could not believe how lucky we were. Three hours later things went wrong – she stopped breathing, and suddenly the storm came. Elsie was rushed to NICU where she spent two weeks. Almost five months on and we have some obstacles to overcome – the biggest being Elsie's upcoming open heart surgery – but we honestly would not change her for the world and are ready to take on anything, with her holding us up and showing us how to be strong.

Kat Hanuscinova & Emma Thomas, mums to Elsie

EARLY DAYS

I didn't know anything...

... about Down syndrome. I had only briefly heard negative things about it, only seen outdated negative terminology and pictures. All I kept thinking as I stared at her perfect face was 'What kind of life would she have? She won't be able to do *this* and she won't be able to do *that*...'

How VERY wrong was I. I knew that moment I looked at her – she was perfect.

We need to make people aware that it isn't as scary as the outdated information says. In fact it is an amazing journey! It may be a different journey, but it is okay to be different.

Things may take that little longer to accomplish but they will get there and it just makes us able to enjoy those little moments and milestones a little longer.

Mali is now three and thriving. She is such a typical girl; bossy, sassy, and so stubborn and determined. She doesn't use many words at the moment but is a pro in Makaton and picks it up so quickly it's amazing. I only wish I knew then what I know now and how lucky we are to be on this different journey. Everyone needs to be positive about Down syndrome!

Jessica Evans, mum to Mali

I always wanted...

...to be a mum but it's quite tricky to achieve that when single and 50 per cent of the vital ingredients are missing! I've been unlucky in love which meant at 39 I was still without a family of my own. I decided to take the plunge and go it alone, and researched IVF with a donor. Miraculously, it turned out my fertility was good and after one round of IVF and one embryo transfer, I found out I was pregnant. Sadly, I lost that baby. A few months later, I bit the bullet again and went for another transfer. I waited anxiously to find out if I was pregnant. When I started bleeding at six weeks, I was devastated. But a week later at my seven-week scan there was a little beating heart on the screen. My very own baby growing inside me - exactly as it should!

A few weeks later, my mum asked me about screening. I remember casually brushing it off, telling myself it would be fine – nothing to worry about. I vividly recall looking at my mum and saying, "To be honest, if I have a baby with Down syndrome, I feel like I can cope with that!" It was such a strange thing for me to say but I look back and think 'WOW!' - it came from nowhere and it was so true! At my 12-week scan, I casually ticked the boxes for screening without really thinking. It was a Wednesday in December 2018. "Your results will be back by Monday," they said. "If you've not heard anything by then, it's low risk!"

Monday came and went, then Tuesday and Wednesday. Then came the call on Thursday. It was an unknown number and as soon as I saw it, I knew. The midwife told me my 'risk' was 1:5. Anything higher than 1:150 was a high risk. I went to see the screening midwife – a delightful lady but blunt with my options. I was advised that the amnio was diagnostic, giving me 100 per cent clarity, and therefore choices. She regaled lots of anecdotes of ladies who had ended their pregnancies due to testing positive for Down syndrome, and my whole world just froze. I desperately wanted this baby - my perfect baby. I couldn't understand why this was happening to me. As a single mum, why me? Surely, it should be someone else; someone with a partner to support them.

I'm an impatient bitch at the best of times and needed to know immediately. I didn't want an amnio so instead the screening midwife recommended I have the NIPT. A day later my friend drove me to Leeds, but before we even left her street, I threw up in her car – an incident I'll never be allowed to forget!

It was a fancy clinic. I paid my £300 and in return there was a huge screen at the end of the bed, where I could see my baby. There he or she was, happily wriggling around! I saw a beautifully forming brain, a strong heartbeat and a big yawn that on the photo looked like my baby was laughing at me – "Oh Mummy, what are you worrying about? I'm just fine!" Due to the presence of a little nasal bone, and an average range nuchal fold, I was told it was highly unlikely the baby had Down syndrome. Also highlighted the fact that my bloods were showing fertility drugs, and mentioned that my age didn't help!

So there it was, probably fertility medication and my age. All a lot of fuss about nothing. I skipped into Christmas knowing all was well; my baby would be fine! Then on 28 December, the phone rang again. It was the clinic. "Your results are back and UNFORTUNATELY it looks like your baby has Down syndrome. I'M SO SORRY!"

I cried all day… and the next day… and then I got my shit together. "This is my baby, it's healthy. I don't need an amnio. I'll just keep going." One of my oldest friends has a cousin with Down syndrome. She came 250 miles just to give me a hug and tell me it would be fine – Why wasn't everyone saying this? My pregnancy had its ups and downs from there on in. Baby was a tinker – I named her thumper because she kicked so much! When she stopped growing and kicking they brought her out.

It's a moment I will cherish forever. My beautiful, beautiful baby girl – Sadie Robyn – arrived four weeks early and weighed 2.3 kilos (5 pounds 1 ounce). She spent three weeks in NICU and came home on oxygen and has done brilliantly. We have our moments, but our worries are minimal in comparison to what others are going through in life. So here I am, approximately a year after all this worry began and I am the proudest, happiest, most blessed single mum by choice. Why me? Because she was always meant to be mine – I'm one of the LUCKY FEW and I'm so incredibly thankful for my PERFECT baby girl.

Sam, mum to Sadie

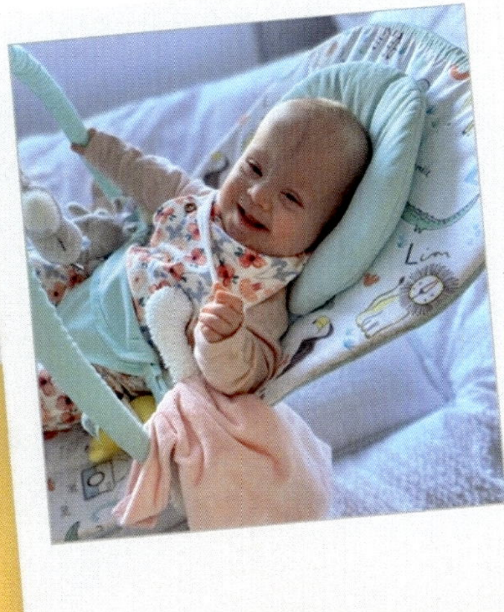

EARLY DAYS

It is unsettling and seems totally ridiculous...

...now as I reflect on the depression and negativity I was consumed with when our second son George was born. He is now seven and alongside his older brother, is the greatest love in my life and the source of all that makes me truly happy.

I am ashamed to say that due to my lack of interest or research I knew nothing at all about Down syndrome before his birth. I had no idea what it may involve as a parent - just that it's top of the list when it comes to eradication and therefore it must be really, really bad.

After a C-section and as relief washed over me, I waited for the joy that was supposed to follow. Instead there was a heavy silence in the room and George was taken away to the special care unit. What seemed like hours later, a very small consultant in a white coat arrived with a giant black frying pan and whacked me round the head with it ten times (as I remember it), by explaining our baby may have Trisomy 21 – otherwise known as Down syndrome.

Whilst I wanted to be with my baby and hold him to make him feel safe, I was also absolutely furious and immediately hated him, and part of me very much wanted to leave him at the hospital.

I was tired beyond words with a demanding two year old at home whom I adored, and who I felt deserved a higher standard for a brother. He shouldn't have this to cope with! He didn't ask for this. I didn't need this! I didn't deserve it and I couldn't do it. I didn't feel in any way equipped to care for a child with additional needs – I really wasn't going to be able to cope. But it was too late – he was here.

This way of thinking haunted me during the first few months of his life. Mostly I think it was – that the thought of how much work and effort it would take to look after him and help him to develop basic skills just freaked me out.

As it turned out George was the easiest baby – he slept like a dream and has never had any major medical issues. The terrible traumas and difficulties didn't materialise and helping him to develop skills has actually been fun and incredibly rewarding.

Once I had managed to relax a little and get to know George, I fell in love with him. Everything he does is impressive and admirable because he is at a slight disadvantage. He loves life – the simplest pleasures, like being offered a biscuit, will make him throw his arms in the air and dance. He attracts a lot of attention because of the joy he presents everywhere he goes, and as a result I think we are all better at talking to strangers.

It makes me uncomfortable to admit that I may have not gone through with the pregnancy if we had had a pre-natal diagnosis, although I believe everyone should have the choice. But how can you make a choice between something you hope for and something you don't realise you might need? Neither of these things ever prove to be what we think.

Our story about George really ends here and I realise it is dominated by those very early days. That is simply because everything is okay now. We are a regular family experiencing the same good days and bad days like everyone else.

All the unhappiness and negativity that surrounded George's diagnosis came from us, George is happy, he doesn't 'suffer' from anything, most of the time he is actually over the moon, and because he is in the world, so am I.

Rebecca Mackay, mum to George

EARLY DAYS

Tania, her husband and two children...

...had not long moved from Pakistan to Cambridge when she discovered she was expecting again.

Within 20 minutes of his birth, the doctor announced that he suspected Down syndrome. Neither I nor my husband had a clear idea of what that meant. My husband and I both shed tears - in shock mostly. I spent the night at the hospital sobbing at the thought of raising my 'disabled' child. The next morning my husband came to me with an email he had composed for family and friends. The email started off with a joyous announcement that our two children now had a baby brother; that mother and baby were doing well, with photos to show how beautiful our new baby boy was. The email then carried on to say that our new baby had Down syndrome. Very casually, it mentioned there were links attached to learn about Down syndrome, for those that weren't familiar with it. This email took a load off me – I had been overwhelmed with how to announce our baby's condition to our large extended family units in Pakistan, who were mostly oblivious to any disability.

Both our families were extremely supportive, particularly from an Islamic perspective. I was told that this baby is Allah's blessing to us; that we were fortunate to have an angel amongst us. As comforting as these words were from family so far away, I still wondered how I would cope. As much as I tried to see our baby's disability as a blessing, I really couldn't.

Soon I was introduced to another Pakistani Muslim woman on Facebook. She had three daughters with a rare genetic disability. These girls were now in their early teens, but were bedridden. Their mother's posts were often accompanied by (with the grace of God) It is an expression of gratitude. I was taken aback by her approach, and asked her what exactly she thanked God for. Her answer resolved my faith as a Muslim. She thanked God for her feet to walk over to her girls, and her hands to attach their oxygen masks so that they could breathe through the night.

I picked up my sleeping baby and laid him on my chest. He picked his head up. He didn't need an oxygen mask to breathe - he needed just love and acceptance from me, as Allah's special little gift .

Allah has selected him to lead us to an exalted position! Not a minute goes by that I don't thank God for my son with Down syndrome. He loves unconditionally, has no expectations, forgives instantly and empathizes instantly...His abilities match no other person I know. He is a perfect human being!

Tania Namia Khan, mum to Qeis

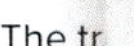

ابتدائی دن

تانیہ ، اس کے شوہر اور دو بیٹے...

اس کا مقابلہ کیسے کریں گے۔ میں نے اپنے بچے کی معذوری کو بطور نعمت دیکھنے کی کوشش کی، میں واقعی میں ایسا نہیں کرسکا۔

جلد ہی میں ایک اور پاکستانی مسلمان خاتون کو فیس بک پر مل گیا۔ اس کی تین بیٹیاں تھیں جو ایک غیرمعمولی جینیاتی معذوری کے ساتھ تھیں۔ یہ لڑکیاں اب نو عمر کی تھیں، لیکن بستر پر سوار تھیں۔ ان کی والدہ کی پوسٹس کے ساتھ اکثر 'الحمدللہ' آتا تھا یہ اظہار تشکر ہے۔ مجھ سے اس کے قریب آکر حیرت کا سامنا کرنا پڑا، اور اس سے پوچھا کہ انہوں نے خدا کا شکر ادا کیا ہے۔ اس کے جواب نے ایک مسلمان ہونے کی حیثیت سے میرے ایمان کو حل کردیا۔ اس نے خداوند کا شکر ادا کیا کہ وہ اس کی لڑکیوں کے پاس چلنے کے ل اس کے پیروں اور اس کے ہاتھوں سے ان کے آکسیجن ماسک لگائے تاکہ وہ رات بھر سانس لے سکیں۔

میں نے اپنے سوتے ہوئے بچے کو اٹھایا اور اسے اپنے سینے پر لٹا لیا۔ اس نے اپنا سر اٹھایا اور میں نے اس کے چہرے پر 'نور' دیکھا۔ اسے سانس لینے کے ل آکسیجن ماسک کی ضرورت نہیں تھی-اسے صرف مجھ سے محبت اور قبولیت کی ضرورت تھی،کیونکہ اللہ کی نگہداشت کے لئے خصوصی تحفہ ہے۔

اس کے بعد سے،میں اکثر کثرت سے الحمد للہ کو دہراتا ہوں اور ساتھ ہی اللہ نے ہمیں ایک اعلی مقام کی طرف لے جانے کے لئے اس کا انتخاب کیا ہے! ایک منٹ بھی نہیں گزرتا ہے کہ میں اپنے بیٹے کے لئے ڈاؤن سنڈروم کے ساتھ خدا کا شکر ادا نہیں کرتا ہوں جسے وہ غیر مشروط طور پر پیار کرتا ہے،اس کی توقعات نہیں ہوتی ہیں،فوری طور پر معاف ہوجاتا ہے، فوری طور پر ہمدردی کرتا ہے اس کی قابلیت کسی دوسرے فرد سے نہیں ملتی جس کے بارے میں جانتا ہوں۔ وہ ایک کامل انسان ہے!

...یادہ عرصے سے پاکستان سے کرمبرج منتقل نہیں ہوئے تھے جب انہیں پتہ چلا کہ وہ دوبارہ امید کر رہے ہیں۔

اپنی پیدائش کے بیس منٹ کے اندر،ڈاکٹر نے اعلان کیا کہ اسے ڈاؤن سنڈروم کا شبہ ہے۔ اس کا کیا مطلب ہے اس کا مجھے اور نہ ہی میرے شوہر کو کوئی واضح اندازہ تھا۔ ہمارے پاس کتابچے اور بروشرز دیئے گئے جس میں بتایا گیا تھا کہ ہمارے نئے بچے کے بولنے کے مسائل/ جسمانی اور ذہنی معذوریوں/دل کی ممکنہ پریشانیوں کے امکانات ہیں۔

زیادہ تر صدمے میں- میں اور میرے شوہر نے آنسو بہائے۔ میں نے اپنے " معذور " بچے کی پرورش کے خیال میں رات کو اسپتال میں روتے ہوئے گزارا۔اگلی صبح میرا شوہر میرے پاس ایک ای میل لے کر آیا جس نے اس کنبہ اور دوستوں کے لئے تشکیل دیا تھا۔ای میل کی خوشخبری اعلان کے ساتھ ہوئی تھی کہ اب ہمارے دونوں بچوں کا ایک بھائی ہے۔ یہ معمول کرنے کے لئے کہ ہمارا نیا بچہ کتنا خوبصورت تھا ، ماں اور بچوں کی تصاویر اچھی تھیں۔اس ای میل پر پھر یہ کہا گیا کہ ہمارے نئے بچے کو ڈاؤن سنڈروم تھا۔انتہائی اتفاق سے ، اس میں ذکر کیا گیا ہے کہ ڈاؤن سنڈروم کے بارے میں جاننے کے لمنسلک رابطے تھے، ان لوگوں کے لئے جو اس سے واقف نہیں تھے۔اس ای میل نے مجھ پر بوجھ پڑا- میں اس بات سے مغلوب ہوگیا تھا کہ پاکستان میں ہمارے خاندانی اکائیوں کے لئے اپنے بچے کی حالت کا اعلان کیسے کریں، جو زیادہ تر کسی معذوری سے غافل تھے۔

میں نے آہستہ آہستہ اپنے نئے بچے کو گرمایا،جوابھی تک مجھ سے ناواقف تھا۔پاکستان سے آئے روز کنبہ کے ممبروں کی روزانہ فون آتی تھی۔ہمارے دونوں کنبے خاص طور پر اسلامی نقطہ نظر سے انتہائی معاون تھے۔مجھے بتایا گیا کہ یہ بچہ ہمارے لئے اللہ کا فضل ہے۔ کہ ہم خوش قسمت تھے کہ ہم میں ایک فرشتہ ہو۔جب تک یہ بات گھر والوں کی طرف سے دور دراز کی بات ہے،مجھے اب بھی حیرت ہے کہ میں

Both my children are a product of IVF

Two weeks before he was born, when we found out that our youngest, Billy – who had been a frozen embryo for two years – had Down syndrome, I have to say I went through a heap of negative emotions. Why me? How could this happen? We are paying thousands of pounds for our children how can they not be perfect? I won't be able to cope, I don't want a 'wonky' baby, my life is ruined. Yes, it really was that dramatic! Now that Billy is ten years old, I can't believe I got it SO wrong. Billy is unbelievable! He is clever, has an incredible wit, and a beautiful soul as well as a beautiful face.

Lucienne Davies, mum to Billy

EARLY DAYS

From 20 weeks pregnant...

...we knew that there was 99 per cent chance that our baby was going to have Down syndrome. Not only that, but would also require open heart surgery, a kidney operation and possibly a birth miles away from home.

I was 21, just turning 22 when I fell pregnant with Gracey. Everything suddenly changed from reading about 'what size my baby is this week' to 'success rates of open-heart surgery'. We were back and forth to Glasgow for months for scans and tests. We were told of numerous chromosomal abnormalities that Gracey potentially had and to prepare ourselves for her only living a very short life. We couldn't take the unknown any longer and decided to have the amniocentesis test. When I received the phone call confirming she had Down syndrome it felt like my whole world just stopped. This was not the family picture I had always dreamed of. I felt extremely guilty as if I had done something that had caused it. I felt horrible for feeling bad about who she was. She wasn't the daughter I had imagined I would have; I wish I had known then that she would be way better than what I had thought I wanted. I spent weeks on end worrying, reading and researching as I had no idea what to expect.

At appointments some professionals made me feel like my life was going to be so difficult! I was told I wouldn't cope, that Gracey won't get much out of life and how limited her life would be, but how wrong they were. Everything they told me about what Gracey would be like scared me, but it turns out these things were all false. It was like they were trying to make my mind up for me, and I spent so much time worrying instead of enjoying my pregnancy.

Gracey is exactly who she was made to be, from the very start. She is nothing like I ever imagined but exactly what I needed. She has been through more than most already in her short life. Gracey has so much joy, and her smile would brighten anyone's day. She is full of life and I am so proud to have her. I wouldn't change her for the world. Down syndrome is a beautiful part of her but it doesn't determine who she is. It's not something to be scared of, she is everything we ever needed. She is our reason.

To all new or expecting families, it's okay to feel guilty and upset, but just know that our babies are special and will bring you the most joy. It might be a little bit of a steeper hill at first but the view from the top makes the climb so worth it.

Shannon Wemyss, mum to Gracey

EARLY DAYS

Shilpa is a paediatrician...

...and was working the day Neil was born.

It was a day like any other day. I took the morning rounds checking my patients. By 4pm I started contracting but my shift was supposed to end at 5pm. My husband was working in the same hospital as paediatric intensivist, so I informed him I was in labour and we went to the labour and delivery ward next door. The obstetrician checked the CTG, which is a tracing of the baby's heart rate with the contractions. It was abnormal, so I was instantly taken for surgery and within the next half an hour we were blessed with a beautiful boy.

Lying on the operatiing table, I took a sigh of relief as I heard his first cry. When I was in the recovery room, my hubby came to me and burst into tears, saying our boy had features consistent with Down syndrome.
I still remember my reaction, "Hemant, it's okay, we were chosen for this."

The next two months was the period of so called 'bad news'. One of the best paediatricians of Mumbai, in one of the best hospitals in Mumbai, told us he was sorry. He said Neil's blood test was positive for Down syndrome – that he might not be able to do certain things, he would require a heart scan, eye tests, hearing tests, physiotherapy, speech and language input and on and on. I do not remember anyone saying "Congratulations!" to me. I felt lost those first few months when my baby was born; I did not enjoy his tiny toes, his tiny grip that said without words, "Stay with me."

I have now been working as a paediatrician in the UK for the last five years. When I deliver babies with Down syndrome, I make sure the first thing I say to all new parents is, "Congratulations!"

Shilpa recommends PADS to her new parents and we are working with her to distribute PADS to new and expectant parents at her hospital in central London.

Dr Shilpa Ambulkar, mum to Neil

शुरुआती दनि

शलि्पा एक बाल रोग वशिेषज्ञ हैं

और जसि दनि नील का जन्म हुआ था, उस दनि वह मुंबई के जाने माने अस्पताल में काम कर रही थीं...

यह कसिी भी अन्य दनि की तरह एक दनि था । मैंने सुबह अपने मरीजों की जांच शुरू की । शाम 4 बजे मुझे प्रसव पीड़ा शुरु हुई, लेकनि मेरी शफि्ट शाम 5 बजे खत्म होनी चाहएि थी। मेरे पत िपीडियाट्रकि इंटेन्सविसि्ट के रूप में उसी अस्पताल में काम कर रहे थे, इसलएि मैंने उन्हें सूचति कयिा क िमैं लेबर में हूं और हम डलिविरी वार्ड गए । प्रसूत िवशिषज्ञ ने सीटीजी की जांच की, जो संकुचन के साथ बच्चे की हृदय गत िका पता लगाता है । यह असामान्य था, इसलएि मुझे तुरंत सर्जरी के लएि लयिा गया और अगले आधे घंटे के भीतर हम एक सुंदर लड़के के साथ धन्य हुए ।

ऑपरेशन टेबल पर लेटे हुए, मैंने राहत की सांस ली जब मैंने उसकी पहली आवाज सुनी । जब मैं रकिवरी कक्ष में थी , मेरे पत िमेरे पास आए और रोने लगे , बोले हमारे लड़के को डाउन सड्रिोम के लक्षण हैं । मुझे आज भी मेरी पहली प्रतक्रियिा याद है, हेमंत, ठीक है, हम इसके लएि चुने गये है ।

अगले दो महीने तथाकथति "बुरी खबर" की अवध िथी । मुंबई के सर्वश्रेष्ठ अस्पतालों में से एक, मुंबई के सर्वश्रेष्ठ बाल रोग वशिषज्ञों में से एक ने हमें बताया क िउन्हें खेद है । उन्होंने कहा क िनील का रक्त परीक्षण डाउन सड्रिोम के लएि सकारात्मक है, वह कुछ चीजें करने में सक्षम नही हो सकता है, उसे हृदय स्कैन, नेत्र परीक्षण, कान की जांच, फजियोथेरेपी, स्पीच थेरेपी और ऐसे कई जांचों की आवश्यकता होगी । मुझे याद नही है की कसिी ने मुझसे कहा हो , "बधाई हो!" बेटा होने के बाद के पहले कुछ महीने मैंने खो दएि ; मैंनें उसके नन्हे नन्हे हाथ पैर की उंगलयिों को महसूस नही कयिा , उसके हाथों की छोटी पकड़, जो बनिा शब्दों के मुझसे कह रही थी , "मेरा साथ मत छोडना ." अब मैं इन नए माता-पताओं के लएि कुछ अलग चाहती हूं ।
आज कई सालों बाद, नील नॉर्मल स्कूल में पढता है और उसकी बेडरूम की दीवार पर कई प्रमाण पत्र लगे हुए हैं.

अब मैं पछिले पांच साल से ब्रटिन में बाल रोग वशिषज्ञ के रूप में काम कर रही हूं । आज जब मैं डाउन सड्रिोम के बच्चों की डलिीवरी करती हूं , मैं यकीनन सभी नए माता पताओं से ये कहती हूं , "बधाई हो! चतिा में समय ना गवायें, आपने नन्हे शशि को मन भर कर प्यार करे ।" इन नए माता पताओं को डॉ शलि्पा PADS की सफिारशि करती है। हम डॉ शलि्पा के साथ मलिकर मध्य लंडन के अस्पतालों में PADS का वतिरण करते हैं।

डॉ। शलि्पा अंबुलकर ने नील को मुखाग्न िदी

EARLY DAYS

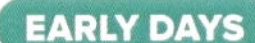

When I look at Amelia...

...I see the most perfect daughter I could ever have wished for. Yes, there are still things she may struggle with, but I am so proud of how strong minded and courageous she is, and every day she surprises me with something new she has learnt to do – small things to everyone else but huge things to us. With her strength and determination there is no stopping her!

Jyoti Budhia, mum to Amelia

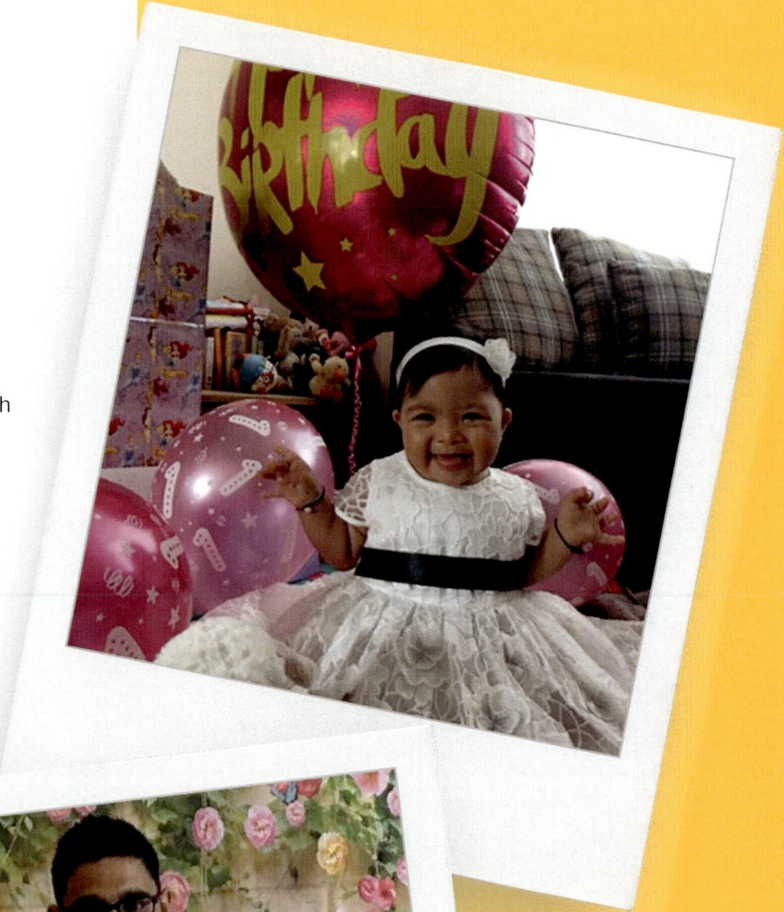

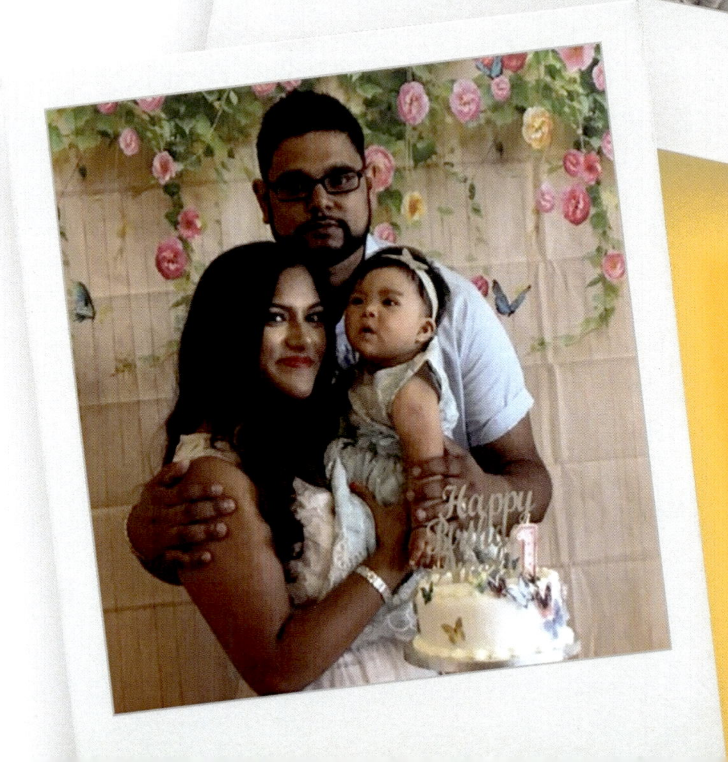

EARLY DAYS

The day after Marcie was born...

...we were told she had markers for Down syndrome. We went into denial, thinking they'd got it wrong but her blood test results came back a few days later and they gave us her official diagnosis: Trisomy 21 Down syndrome.

We asked what that meant for her and we were given an outdated leaflet and were told not to Google anything. That was it. We cried over the 'loss' of our daughter we thought we had and worried about what our future as a family meant now...

Then we rebelled against the doctor's advice. We Googled, we researched, we found Positive About Down Syndrome and suddenly it felt like a weight had been lifted. We weren't alone in this – all these babies, children and adults were incredible and achieving so much. So what were we even worrying about? We might be on a different journey than we expected but we're taking the scenic route and we're loving it.

Marcie is smiley and VERY chatty; loves cuddles, music and books; has Down syndrome; likes to steal my glasses; hates loud sounds (unless she's making them!); loves swimming; loves sharing my morning green juice; and could happily sit for ages just watching you talk and sing to her. Notice how Down syndrome is just a small part of who Marcie is? If only we'd known this when we got her diagnosis, we wouldn't have wasted any time grieving and we would have spent more time celebrating our little something extra!

Holli Sheahan, mum to Marcie

EARLY DAYS

At 22 weeks, after 90 minutes...

...of scanning we were told our unborn baby had a significant heart defect, markers for Down syndrome and was showing signs of hydrops, (fluid collection around organs). We were told the heart could be fixed, Down syndrome was something that not all parents were willing to live with, and hydrops would be fatal. We fell apart.

We were immediately offered a termination. We were adamant, "No!" We were advised to think about it. Again, we said, "NO!" We were told to go home and think about it.

The rest of my pregnancy was chaos. I went from too much fluid to not enough. Jacob went from being very active to spending the last nine weeks in the breach position. Poor doppler readings led to three scans a week but at least the signs of hydrops went away, so that was one less worry.

Three weeks before our due date, we went for a check-up and were told "We have a bed for you and a cot for baby – you aren't going home!" At 5.30pm Jacob was born by C-section and whisked off to NICU.

After three months of rigorous feeding, medication and support from the community team, Jacob had his complete AVSD heart repair surgery. Eight hours without our boy, waiting and praying. We got the call, "All fine, you can come and see him." We didn't recognise our baby boy, swollen from being operated on, with more tubes and wires than we could count. Just two days later Jacob was smiling and laughing, stronger than we could imagine and so much stronger than any of us. Slowly all the tubes and wires were removed, and thanks to the amazing team at Birmingham Children's Hospital, a week later we took our boy home – his heart now properly formed but with two leaky valves which will need future surgery.

Every day since, Jacob has thrived, developed, grown and amazed us. He is doing things we were told he would never do. He sits unaided; he has started standing for a few seconds with no help; and while he hasn't quite mastered crawling, he rolls everywhere he needs to be. He babbles constantly, says 'Mama' and 'Dada', and is unbelievably aware. Even a recent stay in hospital for a bout of pneumonia could not erase his amazing smile, which can charm the birds from the trees. The bond he has with his big brother Noah is a joy to behold. We cannot believe the love we have for our gorgeous boy, he brings us such joy. He is a cheeky little monkey and a right character. His smiley face is what gets us through the tough days.

Having Down syndrome does not and will not ever define him. It is part of him and what makes him so amazing, the same way that his 'zipper' from his heart surgery (as his brother calls it) is a part of who he is. We know there will be challenges ahead – a second heart surgery being one of them – but he's a tough cookie and our warrior, and will no doubt continue to prove people wrong. It's been one hell of a rollercoaster so far but we wouldn't change anything.

Rhea Meanwell, mum to Jacob

EARLY DAYS

Our daughter Thea was clearly determined...

...to make her entrance into the world on her terms. It was slightly unfortunate that we weren't quite prepared for her to do so and she ended up being delivered by my husband, in our car, with the help of a 999 operator on speaker phone! It was oddly very serene and luckily paramedics were on the scene within a few minutes, greeted by two gleeful – if rather bemused – parents and a gorgeous baby girl who was most certainly making full use of her lungs! We should have known then what a determined spirit Thea would go on to have.

It wasn't until we arrived at hospital that the nurse suggested that Thea may have Down syndrome based on some physical signs, and asked whether we had known this was going to be the case. We didn't. I remember looking at Thea and feeling overwhelmed with love, knowing that I would do everything I could do to be her fiercest protector and biggest advocate. I would be lying if I did not say I felt some sadness, although this was more about how society would accept Thea, and how my friends and family would take the news. My heart felt heavy with the thought of having to announce the fact that our daughter had Down syndrome when really I did not want to announce it all – it didn't matter. We spent the next few hours Googling Down syndrome and I kept relaying the list of characteristics to my husband whilst scanning Thea, looking for signs to confirm or deny the Medical professionals' suspicions. I read about what she would not achieve, what health conditions she would have, that she would have a shorter life expectancy, and probably would not get married or have children. Some of it was factual, but as I went on to discover, the majority was based on outdated information.

I really wish I had spent this time soaking up the newborn bubble bliss, and getting to know our new addition who was just hours old. Instead I was overthinking every scenario, and trying to put together a message to tell friends and family of the news we had received, rewriting it over and over again. We needn't have worried; our friends and family were and continue to be beyond amazing. Thankfully Thea was healthy and didn't show any signs of a heart condition, so we were discharged less than a day after arriving at hospital and were excited to introduce Thea to her big brother and extended family. To say our son was overjoyed to meet his baby sister would be an understatement; I've never seen anyone prouder. In fact, he continues to be her biggest cheerleader!

Lenise Christian, mum to Thea

EARLY DAYS

I was 19 when...

...I found out I was pregnant, and I had not given the possibility of Chloe having Down syndrome a second thought. It wasn't until a private 3D scan at 30-weeks picked up on Chloe's AVSD (hole in her heart) when I was given a 50/50 chance of her being born with Down syndrome. In that moment, I felt like my world was falling apart. The daughter I thought I was having had gone, and was replaced with a baby that I thought would not be able to learn, would not be accepted, would not be able to do any of the things parents want their children to be able to do.

My last few weeks of pregnancy were spent worrying over my laptop, Googling 'Down syndrome babies', and asking questions on parent forums. One night I had a reply from another mum who has a daughter with Down syndrome, and I will forever be thankful for her reply. She introduced me to a private support group on facebook for parents in Scotland who have children with Down syndrome. From then, I realised that I was not alone with my fears, and that my feelings at the time were also perfectly natural.

My fears were based on stereotypes and outdated, inaccurate information. As my support network grew, so did my understanding of Down syndrome. Being introduced to other parents in the same situation has been far, far more valuable and eye opening than textbook information.

My advice to parents who have a prenatal or antenatal diagnosis, is to get in contact with your local Down syndrome support groups and join PADS – there is a page for expectant mums and another for new parents. Don't listen to negative comments or advice, however well meaning they may be.

The past six years have been a rollercoaster, and there have been moments that have nott been easy, but surely that defines parenthood in general?

And every day has been so worth it.

It's a cliché, but I wouldn't change Chloe, and I wouldn't change the fact she has Down syndrome, as she just simply wouldn't be the Chloe that I know and love.

I push Chloe to be the best she can possibly be, and I don't let her diagnosis get in the way of that.

She's my little bundle of perfection.

Jade Lennon, mum to Chloe

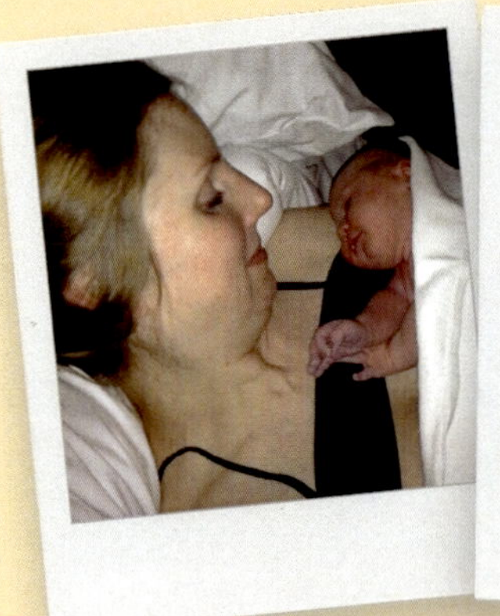
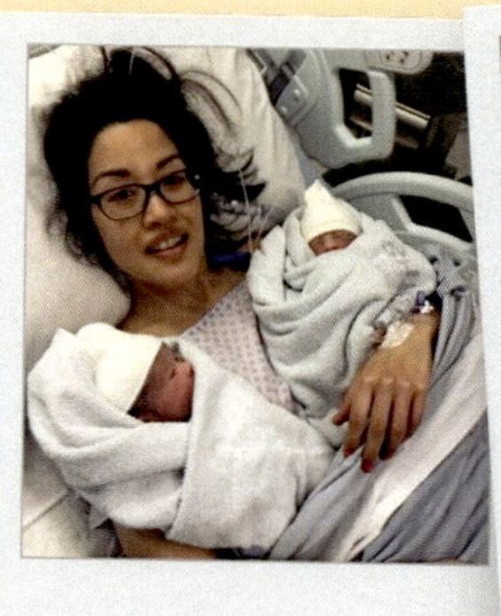
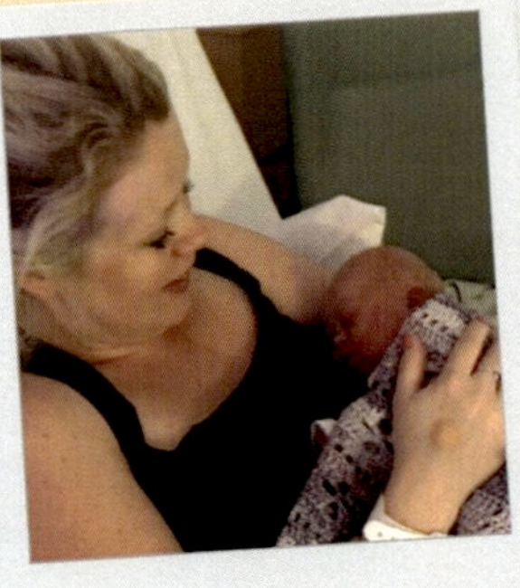
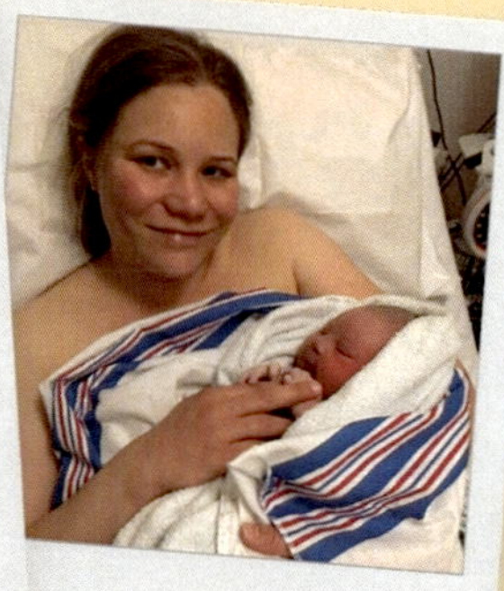
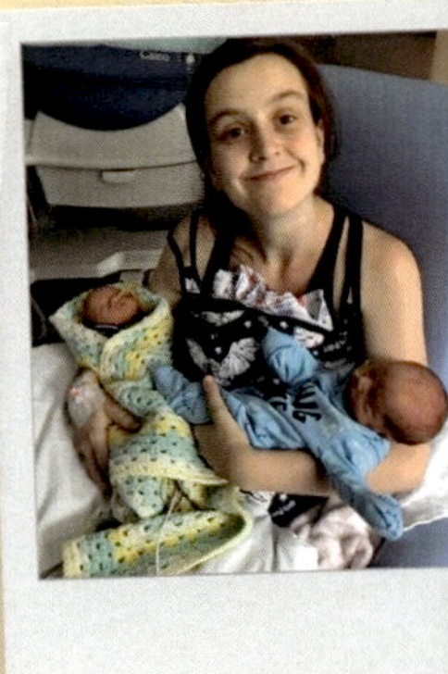

What would I say to myself if I could go back in time?

Stop worrying, thinking and feeling sad about the future. No one knows what's to come for anyone. Hold, cuddle and love this little boy in the moment. Be present right now!

Don't worry about the future, just take things a day at a time, or even one feed at a time in the early days.

Enjoy every moment of your beautiful child. There are going to be so many good times and much happiness along the way.

Your child will teach you so much about the world. Take him home and just love him as you would any child. Love is unconditional.

Don't mourn the baby you thought you'd have, celebrate the one you do have; he will bring you more joy than you could ever imagine.

Stop looking so far into the future, we can't predict it for **any** of our children....Look to the now, feel the love and enjoy being pregnant/your newborn baby.

Don't worry, you've got this and you'll be the mum she needs you to be. She's a fighter; just remember who she gets it from!

Relax, you can both do this.

Just love her, the rest will come.

Put the diagnosis to one side and take that bubba home to love.

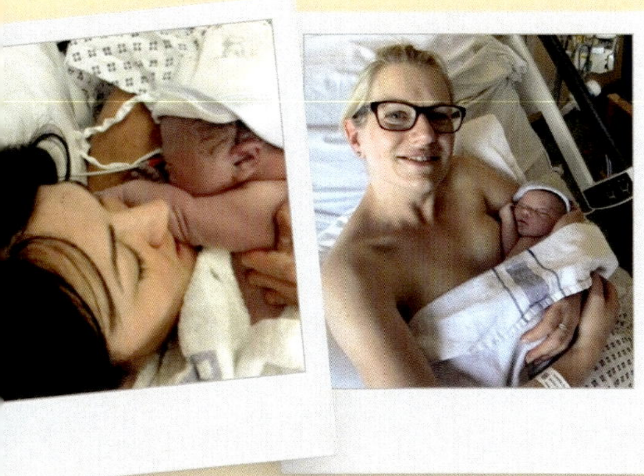
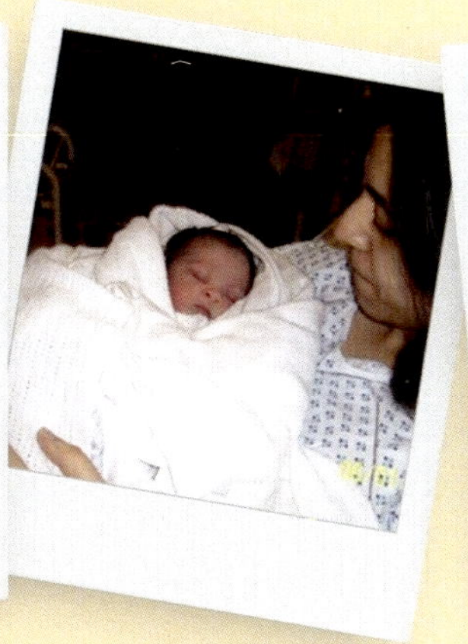
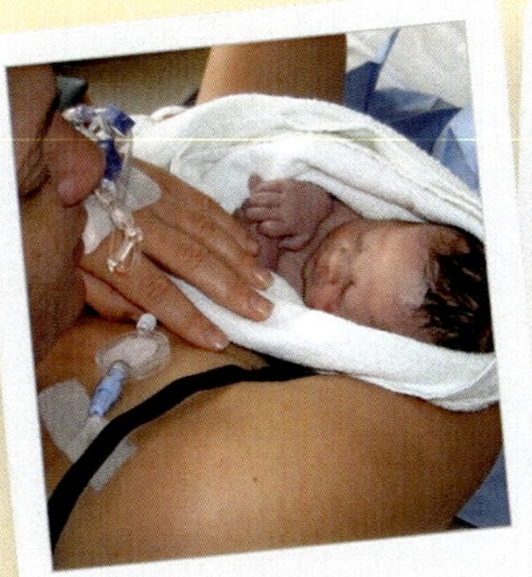
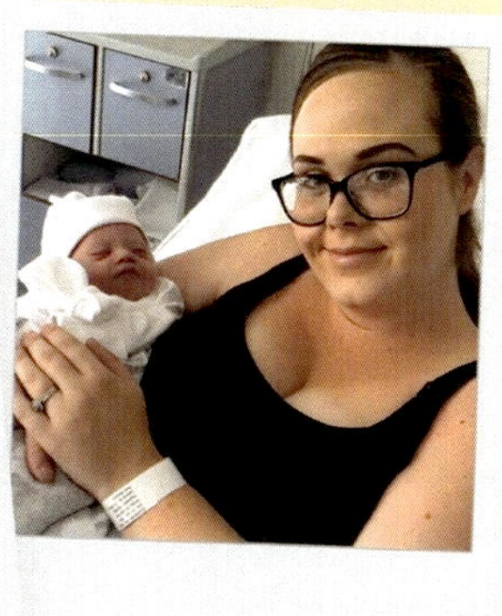

Don't compare your journey with others'. Every child, regardless of how many chromosomes, is different and so is the journey they will take.

Get a grip woman, she is YOUR baby. Of course she is going to be amazing and you will love her!

You got this! You are going to love this little girl so much your heart will burst with joy.

Hold tight, it might get bumpy but we've got this!

Look around and you will find support with your new extended family: your Down syndrome family.

It's going to be a rollercoaster ride with lots of Fun! Fun! Fun! along the way, a lot of education and new lifelong friends. You'll never know love like it and will fight everyone to get what your child needs – it's an adventure that you will never want to end.

Trust in her, she will surprise you. She will overwhelm you with the honesty of her love for you and she will change how you see and experience the world.

He's simply a baby, his chromosome count doesn't tell you what sort of person he will become.

Be prepared to laugh every day!

Come out of the dark place and see her for who she is. She is every bit the daughter that you have longed for.

Sing to her like any other child, play with her like any other child and enjoy her! She's beautiful.

Enjoy every moment with your baby – it goes so fast!

EARLY DAYS

From the moment we laid eyes on Logan...

...it was instant, we were in love with our perfect baby. About 12 hours later we were given our Down syndrome diagnosis and our world felt like it was crumbling – this was not the life we had envisioned for him.

When we had had our Down syndrome test at 20-weeks we had discussed that we would terminate had we had a positive diagnosis, but there we were – he was here and he had Down syndrome.

Little did we know how amazing he would make our lives. We are now both trained in Makaton – along with his Grandma – a skill we would have never thought to acquire. We are part of an amazing community of other parents that offer the most amazing friendship and support. Although our friends and family struggled at first, Logan has now normalised special needs for everyone and is loved for just being himself. Every day he does something else to make us proud, and his smile gives our whole world meaning.

Becky and Charlie Pickering, parents to Logan

EARLY DAYS

Having twins is ordinary...

...but having one twin with Down syndrome is extraordinary. Both our daughters, but especially Ella, have tested our strength to cope with life, our love, our courage, our patience and our perception of life. With our cultural background, we had lots of issues and questions in our mind about how we would handle and break the news to our family and friends back home where Down syndrome was never discussed. We feared what would happen to her and how we would cope. It was difficult to start. However, family, friends, the school, health agencies and the local support group helped us get through our worries and fears. Ella is our 'happy pill' – she brings joy to the family and brightens our day when things get tough. We are so proud of her for making our lives extraordinary.

Myrna and Errol Obaldo, parents to Ella

Ang pagkakaroon ng anak na Downs Syndrome ay di pangkaraniwan .Gaya ng isa sa kambal kong anak na si Ella.Sa kondisyon ni Ella, nasubok ang ang aming pagkatao,katatagan sa buhay,pagmamahal at pasensya. Nadagdag pa sa aming pagsubok kung paano sasabihin sa aming pamilya , kamag anak at mga kaibigan sa Pilipinas ang tungkol sa kondisyon ng aming anak. Nasa amin yung takot at pangamba na di matanggap o madiskrimina ang aming anak sa kadahilanang karamihan sa mga tao ay limitado o walang kaalaman sa kondisyon na ito.

Noong nakompirma ang kalagayan ng aming anak,natakot kami sa anumang pwedeng mangyari sa kanya at kung kakayanin ba namin syang alagaan. Nahirapan kami sa umpisa pero sa suporta ng mga kapamilya,mga kaibigan,mga ibat- ibang ahensya ng gobyerno,eskwelahan lalong lalo na ang Get On Downs, napagtagumpayan namin ang aming takot at mga pangamba.

Si Ella ay nagbibigay sa amin ng saya, nagpapangiti sa mga panahon na kami ay nababalutan ng kalungkutan. Nagagawa nyang bigyan ng kulay ang aming buhay. Ipinagmamalaki namin sya bilang anak at kambal na kapatid.

EARLY DAYS

When Saajan was first born...

...we thought our lives were over as our judgement was clouded with uncertainty. We imagined we'd never travel again, but we've travelled to over ten countries since Saajan was born including our most recent safari adventure to the Masai Mara. We felt like Arjun and Saajan would never have the brotherly bond that we'd hoped for, but they are each other's greatest cheerleaders and comfort. Watching their relationship evolve has been more beautiful than we ever could have imagined! I feared that Saajan would not be welcomed at the Gurdwara (Sikh temple) but my father reminded us of the main teaching of our first Guru, Guru Nanak Dev Ji, that we are all equal and are all God's children regardless of difference. He loves going to the Gurdwara! We had imagined our future to be bleak. Oh how wrong we were!

Three years on, we can safely say that Saajan is the best thing that's happened to our family – he brings all those he encounters so much joy with his infectious smile, and he is often described as a little healer.

Saajan loves motorbikes (like his daddy), eating pizza (like his mummy), playing hot wheels with big brother Arjun, and dancing! He's a pretty easy going guy with a zest for life and appreciation for the here and now, though he is capable of having quite the tantrum!

When he was first born, we had no idea what a beautiful new world our son was about to open our eyes and hearts to. We had a one in 100,000 chance of having a baby with Down syndrome – we hit the jackpot!

Harps Kaur, mum to Saajan

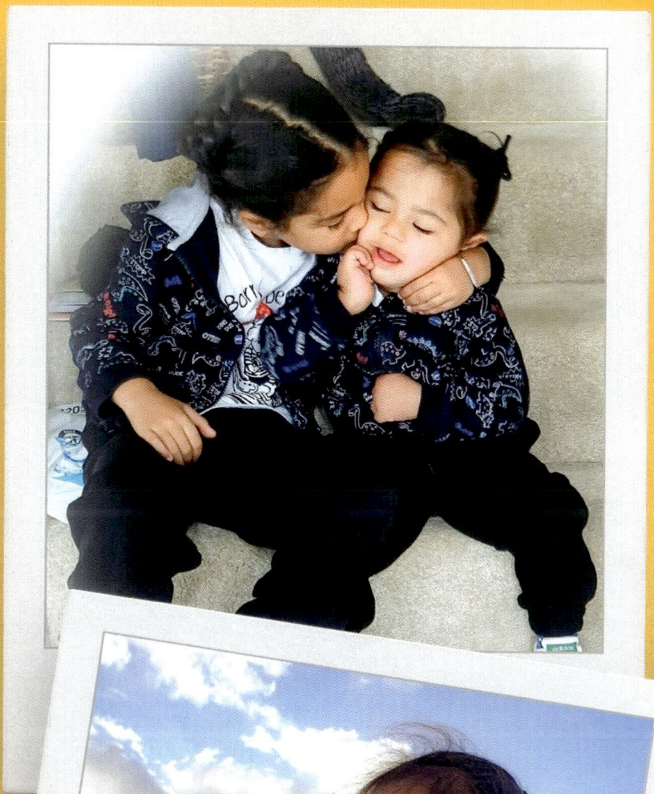

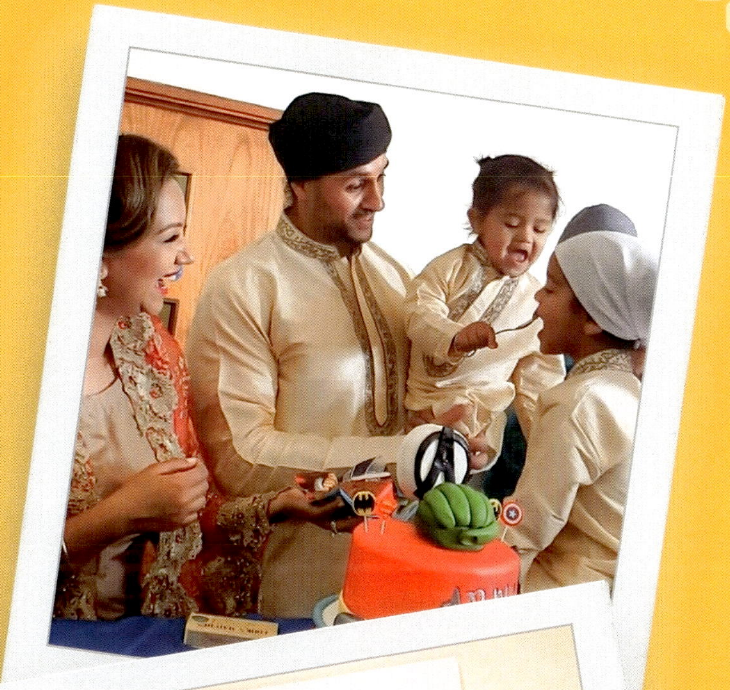

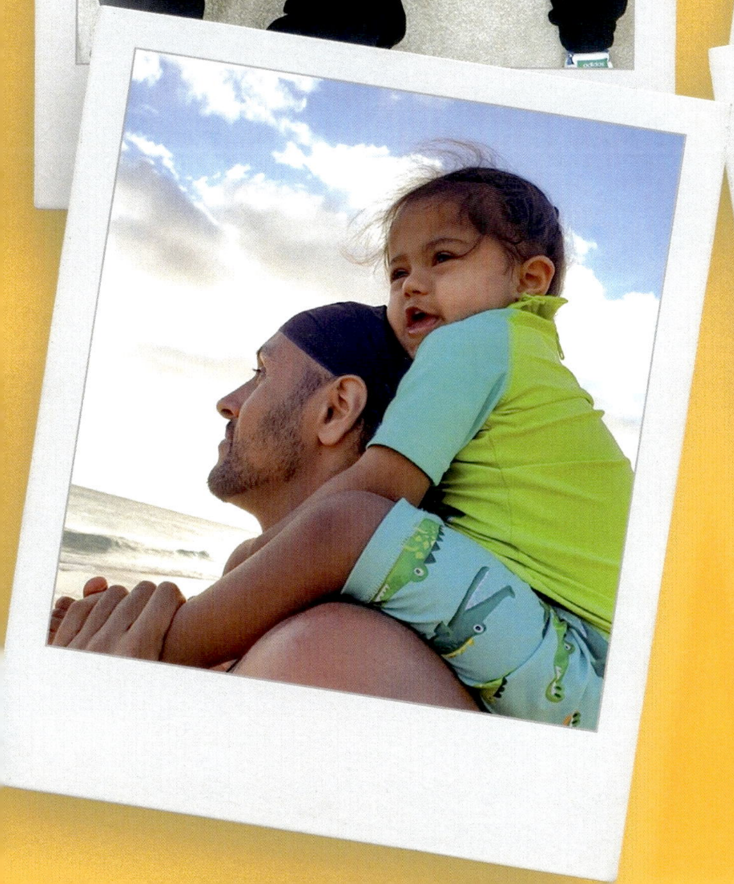

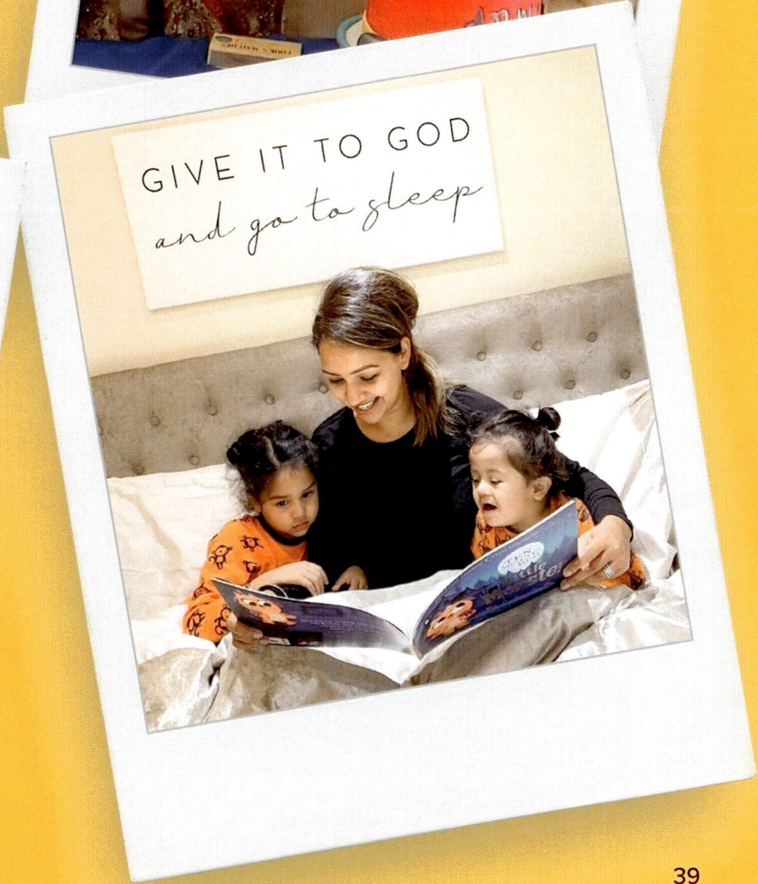
GIVE IT TO GOD
and go to sleep

EARLY DAYS

The moment, shortly after...

...Oscar was born – and we were told by our paediatrician that she was "Sorry" but she suspected he had Down syndrome – will stay with me forever. My heart broke there and then. A mixture of pain, fear and a grief of sorts. I called it grief, as for sometime after, I pined for the baby I always imagined I would have. Mostly it was about me. How it would affect me and my life. How would I cope? This was not how I pictured any of it going. The sadness stayed with me for a long time but then slowly slowly, without even realising, I would wake up every day somehow feeling a bit better than I had the day before, and the fog lifted. I loved him you see. The love had taken over. The truth is, had I known previously – had they detected the Down syndrome prior to birth – I cannot say for certain what I would have done. Of course now I know him, now I see that all those fears in the beginning were so far removed from my actual reality, I would like to think I would have kept him. But I am just not sure. And why? I suppose it would have been that fear again. I had an image in my mind of how I thought people like me would cope or even suffer, and I wonder if I would have made the assumption that it would be awful. I am glad I was not swayed or influenced by health care professionals painting a bleak and dismal picture of what life would look like. Of course life is not without its challenges, but I am just so glad Oscar is here and that he has taught me the true meaning of unconditional, unequivocal love.

Sarah Roberts, mum to Oscar

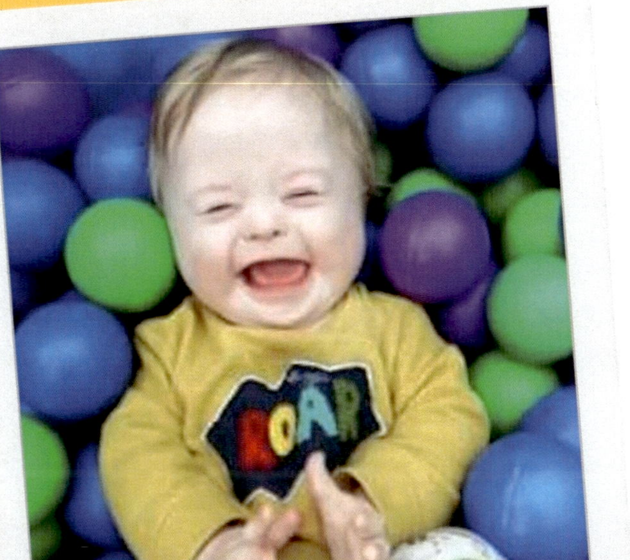

EARLY DAYS

Bertie is an absolute gift!

We absolutely adore him and he brings serenity and happiness not only to us but to literally everyone who meets him. He is developing a cheeky personality and definitely lets us know what he wants!

I am so proud because I really, really struggled with the diagnosis at first. But he is definitely meant to be here and he is my teacher – he's amazing.

Leannder Buttle, mum to Bertie

EARLY DAYS

When we found out...

...we were having twins, I cried. I asked Al, "Why has this happened to us?" When we got our heads around having two babies however, we expected that we would have two babies that we would love and watch grow up to be adults. That was our overall plan and, in that moment when the doctor said they thought the boys had Down syndrome, we realised that the plan had not changed. Life, based on that goal, was going to be exactly as we expected – we would just perhaps be moving along at a different pace during the journey.

Over the past six years, they have developed into charming, entertaining and articulate young men who can liven up any situation. Whilst they have a chromosome count in common, they have completely opposite personalities: one introvert, one extrovert; one left handed and one right; chalk and cheese! Ollie recently said, *"I'm wonderful and so is my brother Cam".* We absolutely agree!

Elaine Scougal, mum to Ollie and Cameron

EARLY DAYS

I didn't know...

...what to expect, there was a real fear of the unknown. It was a fear that things would be so different to my experience with my first child. I was worried about breastfeeding and weaning and going to baby groups. I needn't have worried. Except for extra check-ups and therapy groups, it's all been the same. I've since had twins and Zephy has become the best big brother.

Our experience has shaped our family in ways we couldn't ever imagine.

Sarah Ojar, mum to Zephy

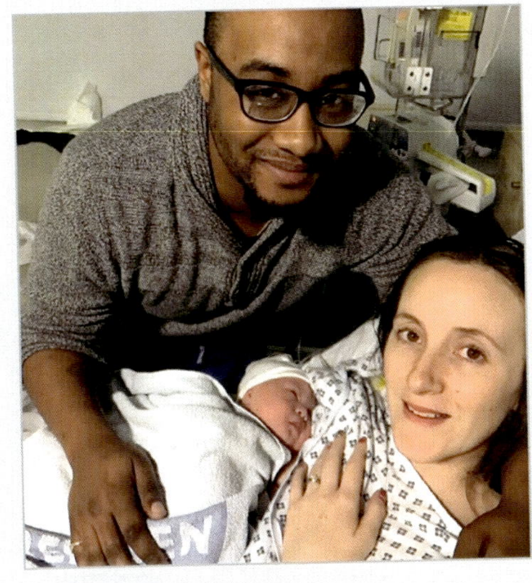

EARLY DAYS

One Wednesday morning I got a phone call...

...that changed our lives forever.

"Your little baby has tested positive for Down syndrome".

Keith and I were devastated. How could this happen to us? I was the healthiest I had ever been and we were 'low risk'.

It was a really dark and painful time for us and it still haunts me that I even considered her life was not worth living. I guess that is what fear and the unknown does to you.

I thank the stars above for giving me the courage to face my fears as four months later the biggest blessing of our lives entered into the world – our beautiful Matilda!

She was absolutely perfect. Everything I could ever need and more.

Linzi Graham, mum to Matilda

EARLY DAYS

We had been trying eight years...

...and after previous miscarriages, I was so relieved when we got past the 12 weeks and thought everything was going to be okay.

Then the test results came back giving a high chance of Trisomy 21 (Down syndrome), but I felt this was my last chance, so I was not prepared to risk another miscarriage.

The wave of guilt I felt that it was totally my fault... We obviously had to talk to each other about the possibility of termination, but in my mind there was never any doubt – there was no way I was getting rid of him. My anxiety was through the roof. I'd think "What if I don't like him?" and feel guilty for having these feelings about my own baby!

Then at 29 weeks, my blood flow was in reverse and my baby was getting no oxygen. He was born weighing just a kilo (2 pounds and 5 ounces), and was smaller than a ruler, covered in wires and tubes breathing for him.

Those feelings I had about not liking him soon went, when I looked at that little face. I thought, "Absolutely perfect, how silly was I?" Reuben had to stay in hospital for three months, he had various blood transfusions and is still on oxygen.

We have been home a year now, with no hospital admissions. Reuben is a little bit behind his peers which is only to be expected, but he is doing fantastic!

Lisa Parton, mum to Reuben

We knew our Beth had a one in two chance...

...of being born with Down syndrome from the combined results of our 12-week scan. The news came like a hammer blow with so many mixed emotions but mostly an overwhelming sense of responsibility. I spent hours Googling the medical conditions often associated with Down syndrome and it felt like we were rolling a dice.

Despite a very healthy pregnancy, Beth was born at 31 weeks as a result of duodenal atresia (a blockage in the bowel) which causes excessive amniotic fluid and often premature birth. The operation to repair the bowel is straightforward and well practised, but as the doctors were preparing her for surgery, it became clear she also had a moderate-size atrioventricular septal defect (AVSD). We did not really have time to dwell as Beth needed surgery, and by the time the news of her heart condition had sunk in she was already successfully back from the bowel operation.

The heart condition meant that Beth was unable to feed orally as she just did not have the energy and coordination to manage breast or bottle feeding. She came home before her due date and was fed my expressed breast milk via an NG tube which went up her nose and into her stomach. We had several appointments with a cardiologist and it was clear Beth would need surgery at around six months old. Our job was to keep her well and fatten her up!

On the morning of the surgery I stayed at home with our two-year-old. My husband signed the consent forms and stayed with her while they put her to sleep, I just didn't have the emotional strength for it. I was by her side as soon as she was back from surgery and stabilised on the Paediatric Intensive Care Unit. The staff at the Royal Brompton were incredible – so knowledgeable, skillful, compassionate and helpful. When I saw Beth post surgery she looked so swollen and I couldn't imagine how she would leave hospital anytime soon. We stayed in the hospital accommodation nearby with our two-year-old and made the most of the excellent care Beth was receiving by treating ourselves to some lovely days out in London, exploring the local sites. We needed that respite from the intensity of the ward and it helped the time pass quickly. Beth was home just nine days after surgery, fully breastfeeding and with no NG tube – it truly was miraculous and life changing surgery.

I wish I had understood and fully appreciated what capable hands my daughter's life was in, because the waiting and worrying was hard. I soon relaxed as I saw her team in action, calmly and expertly dealing with any issue. While this was new to me, they had all seen this before and knew what needed to be done.

Beth is now seven and attends the same school as her sisters Hannah and Jessie, where she is a popular and well-loved pupil and friend. She horserides, swims, loves ballet, enjoys bike rides and sea-kayaking. She even starred in the highly acclaimed BBC drama Call the Midwife! Her life is full of joyful fun which she shares with all she meets, and the only reminder that she was once much frailer is a two-yearly visit to see the cardiologist. She takes no medication for her heart and they do not anticipate that she will require any further interventions - job done!

Sarah Costerton, mum to Beth

EARLY DAYS

I'm new to this...

New to parenthood. New to a T21 diagnosis. New to feelings of guilt, worry and happiness all rolled in to one. I didn't want to join a special group, to be part of a minority fighting my child's corner, perhaps looking at continuous 'intervention' throughout her life. To post things on social media about the progress of my child in the hopes she appears 'normal'. My beautiful child had an amazingly bright future: he would perhaps run a business, marry, have children. But all my expectations and dreams for her were gone the moment her T21 was confirmed.

Sophia was born in the small hours of a March morning in 2020. Just after the world went into lockdown. I had a long and difficult labour resulting in a forceps delivery. She was briefly placed on me and I was so euphoric and exhausted that I didn't notice that they whisked her off far too quickly. In my delirious drugged state (a far cry from my birthing-pool plan with minimal drugs) I was wheeled to recovery and then to a private room on the postnatal ward. I was so out of it that time didn't register. I woke around 6.30am wondering where Sophia was. I couldn't feel my legs.

Sophia was in special care being monitored as her oxygen levels awere low. An X-ray her after birth had shown a slightly enlarged heart. I was wheeled to see her lying in her oxygen tank: this tiny, swollen and battered little human being that I had carried for nine months. A wonderful pregnancy with no issues; low risk. I didn't opt for the screening. I was blasé – it wouldn't happen to me, what were the chances? I was only 34.

I also knew that I couldn't have terminated, even with high chance of T21, having suffered a missed miscarriage at 12 weeks the previous year. It was only a percentage chance anyway and I knew it would cause me stress throughout so I just didn't do it. Ignorance is bliss, after all. My 20-week scan showed up no abnormalities.

Then came the news when Sophia was three days old. We had been carefully managed the previous two days to ensure we started to see the markers for ourselves. A gap between the big toe and the little perfect toes, a slightly flattened bridge of the nose, almond-shaped eyes and, of course, their ultimate concern: a possible heart issue. The machines beeped at us as we sat there

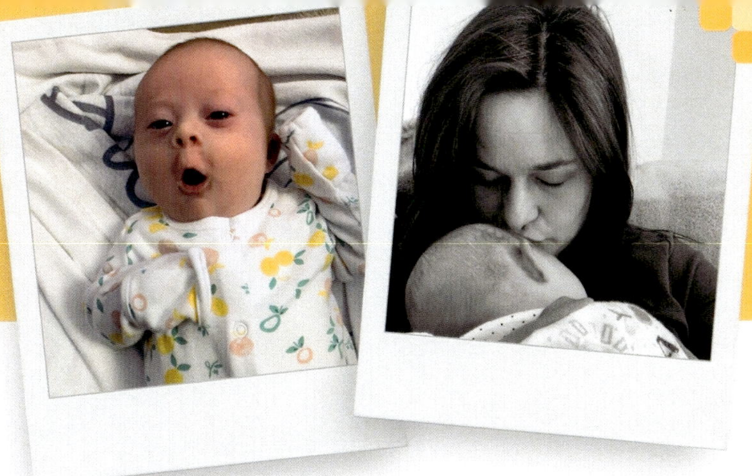

trying to take it all in. She was my daughter and I felt a fierce protection of her already, even though I couldn't see any resemblance to the child I had pictured in my head. That child was gone. I didn't recognise this swollen tiny being in front of me. Black and white print-outs on cheap hospital paper were handed to us as we took it in. Sophia was going to have a list of disabilities and potential health issues. Andy, my fiancé, and I were left alone together to absorb this new information. We held each other so tightly. It was a bad dream. I was back in the kitchen at home, pregnant, with the dogs, looking forward to the birth of our baby girl. This wasn't real.

I struggled to go down and face her – as though I felt like I had betrayed her with my thoughts. I was her parent and I was supposed to fight her corner no matter what. I knew she was due a feed and I wanted to breastfeed despite being told it would be difficult – she had been bottle-fed while I was recovering. I struggled to walk down the long corridor but something inside me overrode my feelings of discomfort. I had to see her.

She latched on immediately and fed for 15 minutes solid, squeaking as she swallowed. She looked at me as she suckled, and I fell deeply and madly in love with her. She was a baby. She was my baby.

On her discharge, we found out that she had no issues with her heart. I burst in to tears at that news, much to the surprise of the lovely Spanish cardiologist. Sophia had a normal, new born heart. She had normal, new born needs.

I have done so much research I don't think I can read any more. Some of it scares me, some of it inspires me, like some of the stories in this book. Nicola's TED talk struck a chord as I realised that she had experienced feelings similar to mine. It's given me the confidence to write this piece. So thank you, Nicola. You were so brave.

This still isn't easy, and I still cry sometimes but as every day goes by I gain more confidence in my new role. I cannot begin to say how much we love Sophia already. I don't want my little girl to be put in a box, though. I want to give her everything I can and help her develop to the best of her true abilities. My fiancé has been amazing throughout. He asked me to define normal; I couldn't. He asked me to tell him who had a perfect life. I couldn't. He thinks the world of her.

Since we've come home, I have watched Sophia develop. She has reached every 'normal' milestone and more. She interacts, she follows me with her eyes, she holds her head up a lot, she pushes on her legs. She holds her rattle. She smiles. I have never seen anything quite so beautiful as that first time she genuinely smiled straight at me.

Vicky Diggens, mum to Sophia

Dear Stork

I am contacting your head office at Stork to give you some feedback on your misleading product messaging with regards to your Special Child™ model.

When we were unexpectedly delivered a Special Child™ from the Down syndrome range, my husband and I were somewhat taken aback and concerned about the future, due to the widespread belief that the extra chromosome feature was going to be a 'bad thing' for our new baby and indeed our family.

However, almost immediately, we were constantly reassured that 'they' were very loving and musical.

Sure, he likes music, but he is yet to show an aptitude for the cello or other instrument – an occasional outburst of Gangnam style in the supermarket is more his forte.

We were also given to understand he would be like all the other children from this range – always enjoying a sunny disposition.

I must inform you, Stork, that this is factually incorrect, indeed as our Special Child™ enters his teenage years he has been exhibiting far too many emotions for our liking. He is stroppy beyond the pale, and has an independent streak that flies directly in the face of your 'A Child Forever' strapline.

A hugger he is not. His flat refusal to reciprocate an embrace on demand from members of the general public has caused us frequent awkwardness, I can tell you.

He clearly has his own opinions, ideas and attitudes which is most perplexing – we were told he would be an 'angel sent from God' and whilst the original manufacturer of our Special Child™ is not necessarily in question, his performance is.

Furthermore, our Special Child™ can be downright naughty, and more often than not, behaves like an actual child. We know from personal experience, also being blessed with a couple of bog-standard models, how nonspecial and rather typical the Special Child™ actually is. We don't wish to complain further but feel it worth mentioning that the bog-standard ones can be far more demanding and yet bring in no income, let alone any perks.

More than once your branding led us to believe that 'they' all look the same. Well let me tell you, Storky, we have met many others and the ridiculous stereotype your marketing team is peddling has proved wrong with alarming regularity. Each Special Child™ looks far more like their parents than others from this range; we are amazed that your board approved such poppycock, and suspect Trading Standards would take a strong view on this.

We did wonder if he may be faulty but upon inspection he appears to have all his working parts and is in absolutely perfect condition.

Another issue that we feel we simply must address is the notion that 'they' are given to 'special parents'. My husband and I are yet to receive any superpowers and have frankly given up waiting for the arrival of our capes. (I would have liked something in purple crushed velvet with gold fringing, if you have any influence in the apparel department). Whilst Mr. EJ has his moments, I must stress that we are just ordinary folk living rather ordinary lives, and although superpowers would not go amiss for all the children, the lack of the cape hurts the most. But I do admit that the odd theme park fast-pass does ease the pain.

Our final point to raise is the incorrect information regarding siblings – ours appear to completely adore the Special Child™ and find him a great source of fun; not remotely burdensome as we were led to believe. The incessant giggles between them and the impromptu party atmosphere over the arrival of cheese on toast is consistently positive.

Whilst we do not wish to return our 'special' bundle – let's face it, the Blue Badge parking is far too handy – we do feel that much of your branding and marketing contravenes British advertising standards.

May we suggest you rebrand this line simply as 'Child™' to avoid the unnecessary negative connotations, head tilting and incorrect expectations that the superfluous title of 'Special' infers?

I look forward to your earliest response to resolve this matter.

Yours sincerely

Confused of Cornwall

P.S. I'm about 5 foot 6 inches, so I would think a modest waist-length cape should be adequate for the school run, non?

Angie Emrys-Jones, mum to Ted (aided and encouraged by Nicola Enoch, mum to Tom)

#MoreAlikeThanDifferent

Toilet Time

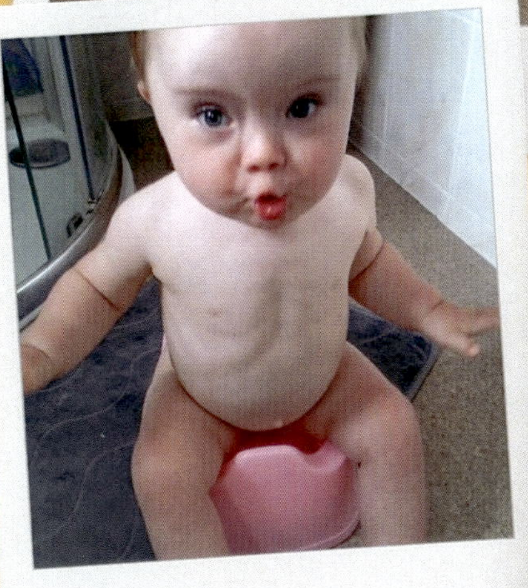

Family

Parents may be concerned about the impact a child with Down syndrome will have on the rest of the family. Our experience and researched evidence show that the family member with Down syndrome is much loved and valued; bringing a whole new dimension to many families and who we wouldn't be without!

FILA

FAMILY BROTHERS AND SISTERS

Our biggest fear was...

...how a baby with Down syndrome would impact on our other children's lives.

Would they suffer because of it?

Would a disabled child stop us doing all the things we enjoyed doing as a family? Days out, holidays, trips to theme parks or a simple walk to the lakes?

Would they resent having a baby who needed so much of our time and attention?

When Jaxon was born, we explained to them straight away. We explained that he would have additional needs, that he would stay a baby for longer. They could not have adored him more.

There has never been any jealousy or resentment. We still do all the things we used to do only it is all the more fun having Jaxon to enjoy it with.

My fears were completely unfounded.

They are so proud of him, and it has brought us even closer as a family.

Lorraine Buckmaster, mum to Jaxon

FAMILY BROTHERS AND SISTERS

Beth & Sara...

Beth: When we were younger I did not realise that other people's experience of disability or diversity was different to mine, but I am proud that Sara has taught me all I know about being respectful, thoughtful and accepting of diversity. While my research and practice now focuses on disability and diversity, my childhood was perfectly 'normal' to me, and mine and Sara's relationship continues to be loving and filled with happiness; I would not change it for the world.

Sara: Growing up was always great fun. When we were younger I learnt so much from her and maybe Beth learnt a lot from me too. When she was young I did all I could to look after her, and as we have grown up she has always supported me in all I do. Both of us have ended up working in jobs that make a difference to help others with learning disabilities. I always enjoy spending time with Beth as she is my 'rock' and my very best friend.

BROTHERS AND SISTERS

I was sadly told...

...by a family member that I was being selfish and ignorant to Harry's siblings by having a child with Down syndrome. That could not be further from the truth! His brothers and sister adore him, watching them play together has shown me true unconditional love. He brings so much happiness to our family.

Marlene Bute-Roper, mum to Harry

FAMILY BROTHERS AND SISTERS

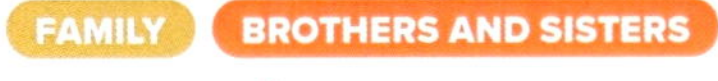

Amelia and Ava

Amelia: I love her so much even though she can be crazy-annoying at times. Like when she wakes me up before my alarm and says “Breakfast, Millie!” – she teaches me patience.

Ava: I love Millie because she is funny, silly, and she loves me, and she looks after me when Mummy and Daddy go out. I love her!

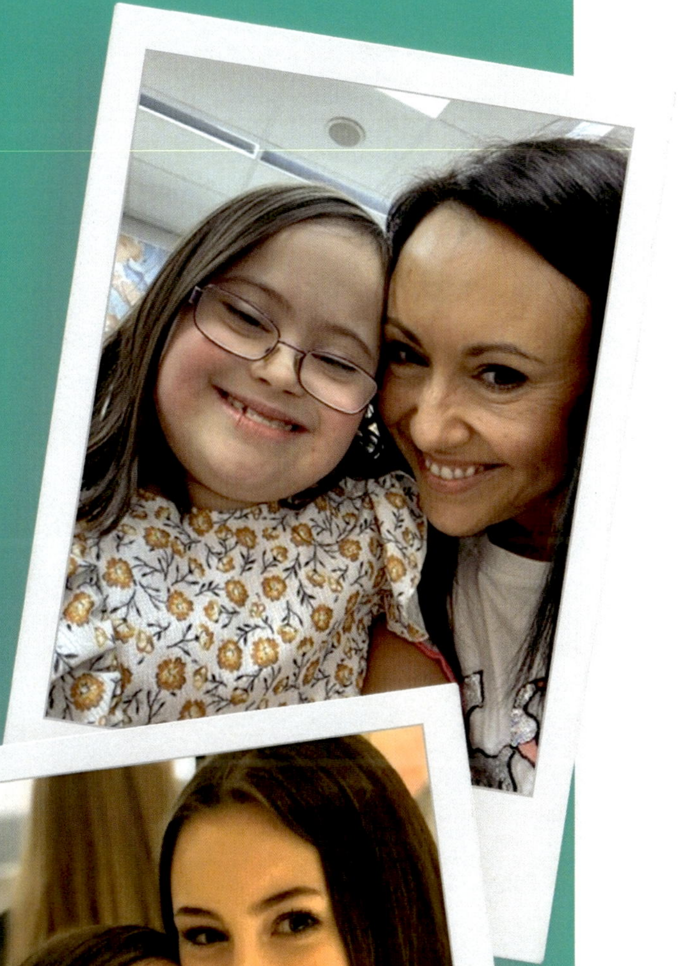

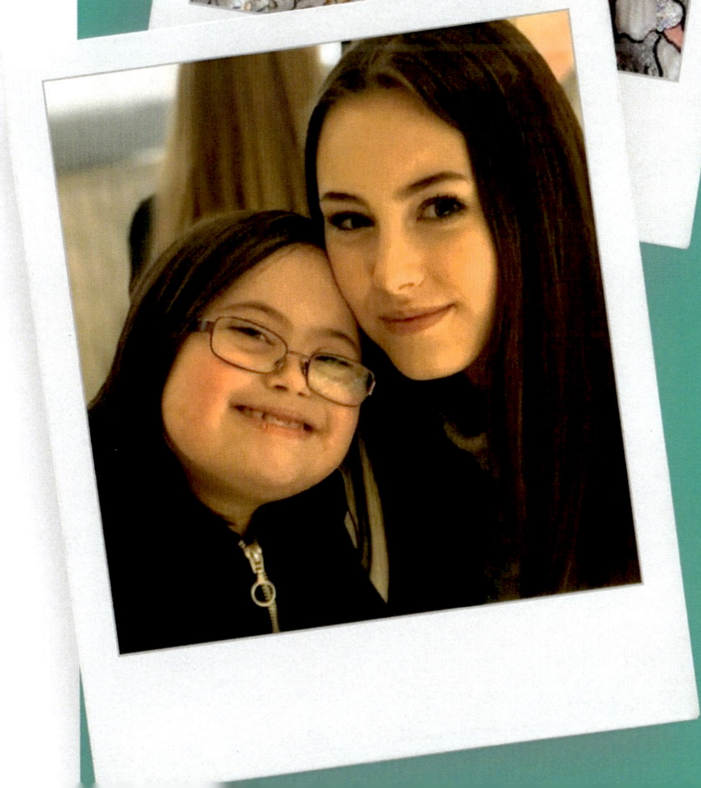

FAMILY BROTHERS AND SISTERS

As a big sister, I cannot imagine...

...life without Gabbie, I do not know what I would do without her. She is now 18 and she is the most amazing young lady. She has become my little best friend and she really is the most caring, loving, kind, stubborn and funny girl. She has achieved so much; so many things that doctors and society are telling us that children with Down syndrome will 'never be able to do'.

She lives her life to the maximum and has an amazing social life – far better than any of her family! She plays netball, rugby and golf; swims; and is in the athletics team. She has a weekly girls' night with her friends. Honestly, she is the happiest little lady ever, and her life is a million miles away from what society portrays. We need to get rid of these outdated opinions and negative images we see on the internet.

She has taught us all so much, me especially. That no matter what, she is still a normal young lady who wants to have the best life and she absolutely can if we give her the opportunity. She has so much to look forward to in the future and I would always do anything I could to help that because that is what she deserves. I have faith in her getting herself a job and living on her own – although I will try and get her to live with me!

Gabbie is my absolute favourite little human, so pure. I am so proud to be her big sis. Never in a million years would I change her.

Megan Kiely, sister to Gabbie

FAMILY BROTHERS AND SISTERS

I have absolutely no negative...

...things – memories or otherwise – to say about Andrew. From the minute he was born I have loved him unconditionally. Seeing the world through Druffle's eyes (as he is affectionately known) is both humbling and eye opening.

He is brilliant on his Playstation and 'takes the Mickey' out of me because I cannot even turn the bloody machine on!

We insult, torment, argue, disagree and name-call like any siblings, and he is without doubt the best brother in the Universe!

Julie Storey, sister to Andrew

FAMILY BROTHERS AND SISTERS

My twin sister Alice...

...is just great. She is the happiest person I have ever met despite the fact that she has a disability. It is just great having someone like Alice in my life.

My first memories of Alice are probably from when I was about two to three years old. I remember Dad would pretend to be asleep on the couch and Alice would give him a kiss to wake him up and then run away laughing.

When I was younger, I felt that Alice got a lot more attention than me. When I was about seven years old, I began to understand that she needed a lot more support to learn things like walking and writing.

As we grew up, I started to notice that when we went out people would sometimes take a second look at Alice or stare at her. I felt they were not nice people and they did not understand Alice or disability. I started to find it tricky to communicate with Alice as she doesn't use much speech and I didn't understand that then. Now we can communicate much better using Makaton.

Now in our teens, Alice and I have got a lot closer and it really is great as we never have arguments or fall out I have my own group of friends and they all take time to say hello to Alice and see how she is doing at school.

I have learnt from Alice to value everybody no matter how different they may be. Alice will always find the sad person in a situation and try to make them feel better.

Although we are twins, Alice and I are very different in terms of our abilities, but there are special times when we can just be the same – such as playing with our black Labrador Harpo, or diving for sticks in the pool on our summer holidays.

Having Alice as a twin sister is probably the best thing that has happened to me; I have learnt to understand about diversity and the world so much more. Alice brings fun or magic to my life almost every day – like when she explodes with delight when we have ice cream for pudding!

Joe Glennon, brother to Alice

BROTHERS AND SISTERS

I was two when my brother was born...

...I used to feel nothing but love for my brother when he was a baby. But as Matt grew up and got into everything, he became annoying – not because of his Down syndrome, just because that is what little brothers are like!

He used to be so embarrassing and do things that made me not want to be seen with him. I knew it wasn't his fault, just me being an awkward teenager.

He is brave and funny and knows exactly what he wants. And he doesn't care what others think of him! He is just happy being himself.

He has shown me that everyone is amazing, whatever their ability. And because of him, I now work as a teaching assistant with kids with additional needs. He has made me more patient, kind and understanding; and a better person for it.

Rachael Coppins, sister to Matt

I was introduced to...

...my cousin once removed, Kevin, when I was 11 years old.

I had been sent to Coventry, literally, for a 'holiday' while my father was dying in hospital.

Kevin made a huge impact on me. He was a lively five year old and he had Down syndrome. He had little speech but an engaging personality and I was totally enamoured.

I later learnt that his mother had been much maligned by her husband's family. They insisted that as there was no history of Down syndrome in their family it was obviously 'her fault'.

Undaunted, his mother insisted on keeping her baby.

Fast forward 30 years when my husband Patrick and I decided to expand our family via the adoption route. We already had two children born to us.

We wanted to adopt a child as young as possible, but while visiting Family Finders in Hertfordshire, we saw 'adverts' for babies with Down syndrome needing homes. I remembered Kevin and it became clear that this was something we could do.

Adam joined our family as a one-year-old in 1993, followed two years later by six-month-old Jessica.

Sadly Jessica died at the age of two following complex heart surgery.

Sophie came to us at six months old. She completed our family and is about to have her 21st birthday.

It has been a rollercoaster ride over the years: frustration, joy, love, exhaustion, worry – but so worth it.

I am so grateful to Kevin's parents, who had the courage to love and care for their child in the face of so much animosity – who then lived until his fifties after having been told that he would not survive childhood.

Adam, 27, is a model, actor and dancer - embarking on a nationwide dance tour. He is also a Special Olympic Gold Medalist.

Sophie is a college student, singer and a Special Olympic Silver Medalist.

I am sad for their birth families, who have missed so much, but very grateful we have Adam and Sophie in our lives. Never forgetting our beautiful Jessica (RIP)

Bernadette Wild had children of her own, before adopting Adam, Jessica and Sophie.

MARATHON
AC101
1079

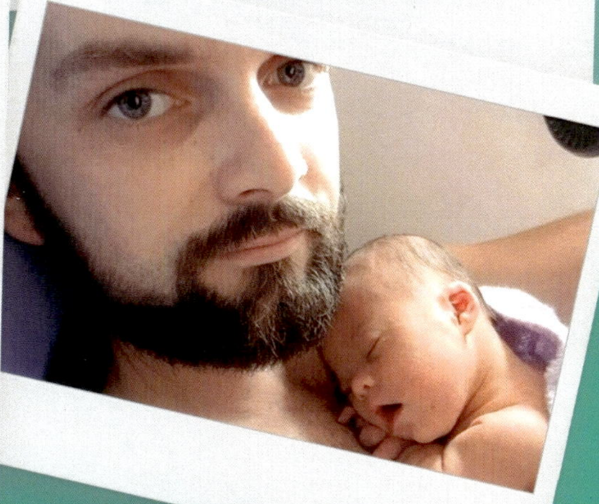

FAMILY DADS

Having Faith has been...

...one of the best decisions in our lives. She is such a cheerful little girl, always with a smile on her face and a song on her lips.

She brightens up my day, I look forward to coming home to see her, to give her a hug whilst listening to her babble even though I have no clue what she says (I guess she is telling me about her day)!

Working full-time can sometimes be challenging to make appointments and give Faith the time she deserves and demands.

You worry all day that you are not being a good parent by working full-time and leaving her with strangers! You second guess yourself, asking if you are doing the right thing!

All these worries disappear when you go in to see her and see that she is the boss, ordering everyone around and totally loving being the centre of attention!

This gladdens my heart and fills me with joy. Even though there have been sleepless nights, nights and days in hospital, days off work, I have no regrets and will always be grateful because we love her to bits.

Segun Obafemi, dad to Faith

FAMILY DADS

It's been one whole year since...

...your brilliant, dramatic entrance into the world. And one whole year since a consultant sat by our bed and told us that he had bad news, that you had Down syndrome. News that changed our whole universe and, I am sad to say now, that we didn't take very well in those first few hours. Mummy was numb and silent, I was devastated, and we had no idea how to tell everyone that suddenly you weren't the baby we thought you were. Honestly Albie, it was such a performance, you'd have thought we were all mad. Because of course you were the same. You were still that wriggly little roly-poly that mummy had carried around everywhere she went for nine months, who waved and yawned in your scans, and who kicked just hard enough that first time so that I could feel you, because you knew I'd been so desperate to know you were there. You'd been giving us nervous butterflies since the day we found out you existed, so how did you suddenly become so scary? You weren't scary, it was us who were scared of the unknown. You are the funniest, bravest, cheekiest little boy who brings us all so much joy. And you are perfectly, unapologetically, exactly who we thought you were all along – our Albie.

Adam Dunville, dad to Albie

FAMILY DADS

Whilst I was away with the military...

...we got the news that Emma's 20 week scan revealed excess fluid on our daughter's brain. I was in shock and had no clue what this meant. Even after it had been explained I think I was even more confused. How could this happen?

We later found out, after having an amniocentesis, that our little baby had an extra chromosome. I didn't know what to think. How disabled would my little girl be? Would she be deformed? Would she be able to do anything normal? Needless to say, it scared me. We already had a child with additional needs; could we deal with another? What would our lives be like?

With me still away at this point, Emma had to deal with pressure from doctors to terminate the pregnancy. They were adamant that Jaimie would not have a fulfilling life and that the best option would be to terminate. Part of me wanted to agree with them – after all they were the professionals and they should know what they are talking about. But after learning that if we terminated, Emma would still have to go through with giving birth to a stillborn child, we knew that wasn't an option.

So obviously we chose to continue with the pregnancy, but the doctors went on to offer us termination 15 times even up to the day we were due to be induced. The way the doctors were pushing us to go the way they wanted, and the pressure that they put on Emma to make decisions whilst I was away, was disgusting and nothing I would have ever expected from the NHS. I had no idea that if your child has Down syndrome you can legally have a termination up until the baby starts traveling down the birth canal. This to me was sickening. I remember thinking, "who in their right mind would go through nine months of pregnancy and then say, maybe this isn't the right choice?" It clearly said in Emma's notes that we had refused termination and that should have been the end of it.

The day Emma was induced, medical staff were on standby ready to perform an emergency shunt procedure on Jaimie's brain, but the worst-case scenario that the doctors were trying to push on us could not have been further from the reality. She didn't need the shunt. Jaimie does have some minor medical issues but absolutely none of them would have warranted the worry and confusion that the doctors caused.

Jaimie is now almost 5 and is one of the most loving children you could ever meet. She is extremely funny, sassy and makes me so proud every day. Yes, she is behind in some areas, but she is so determined and so eager to learn that we have no doubt that she'll achieve everything she sets out to. She will get there when she is ready and every milestone she hits just makes us more proud of her. I wouldn't change a thing and I sometimes forget that she has Down syndrome at all. Then her infectious smile lights up the faces of everyone around us and I remember that she isn't like everyone else. I watch the shock in people's faces as they hear her politely thank them for holding a door open or apologising for getting in the way. People watch in awe as she confidently counts to 10 before shouting "ready or not, here I come" and proceeds to try to find her big brother.

People expect so little of her and are pleasantly surprised when she boldly gives them a "hello" and a cheeky smile. She stands out wherever we go for all the right reasons. I once worried that people would stare with judgemental eyes but instead, I see them look at her with delight and amazement. I love that she has the power to break people's misconceptions just by being herself. Why try to fit in when you were born to stand out? Jaimie and Logan absolutely adore each other and at times they annoy me like any other child would ,but the unconditional love that Jaimie gives makes every day so much brighter.

Steven Mellor, dad to Jaimie

FAMILY DADS

I am Sader Issa...

...a Syrian dentistry student, and the son of a man with Down syndrome. Happy memories are all that I have with my father. As a child I grew up with a man who knows only to love, and a man who worked hard so I can have a normal life. He pushed me to study hard, to be on top of my class so he can be proud of me as I am proud of him.

It is a beautiful adventure to live with a person with Down syndrome. You can learn from them how to love, give, and spread happiness without anything in return.

I am very proud to be the son of that man and I hope that one day your kids with Down syndrome can be parents too.

Sader, son to Jad Issa

My partner and I had...

...a completely "normal" pregnancy. It wasn't until Aurelia was born that we found out she has Down syndrome along with a complete AVSD. It came as a massive shock to us both and we definitely took some time to come to terms with it. I won't pretend it was easy, however we wouldn't change Aurelia at all and it has opened our eyes to a whole new world and way of thinking. Aurelia had heart surgery at the age of four months. This was very difficult to cope with but it's important to have a strong support group around you and it's even more essential not to bottle up your emotions and to actually speak to family, friends, doctors and nurses if you have any questions! It's almost exactly a year now since Aurelia's operation and she has me in stitches every day with her cheeky nature! She is so strong, brilliant and clever!

Matt, dad to Aurelia

FAMILY DADS

We didn't find out...

...Katie has Down syndrome until she was born. Initially I was nervous as to what the future held. The first six months were difficult but after her heart surgery was done and her feeding tube was removed I tried not to treat her any differently than our other two children. I'll be honest and say I spoil them all equally!

At nine months she could say "Hiya" and would say this when I came in through the door. Now she can say lots of words and comes to the door saying "daddy home" when I come back in my van. She loves cuddles and fun and loves reading stories and can say her prayers out loud with me at night.

If I'm going through photos on my phone and I come to her picture it brings a smile to my face every time.

My fears when she was born are all gone and I just love my little girl who loves lippy kisses and playing tag around the kitchen. Her brother and sister love her fiercely and they have lots of fun and good times together.

Nicky Murphy, dad to Katie

FAMILY DADS

My daughter Rachel...

...was the first person I had met with Down syndrome. Her extra chromosome was a surprise to us when she was born in March 2000 and, looking back, I really was already an embarrassing dad. All I could think of was what lay ahead, or what I thought lay ahead, for me and my family.

But nobody told me that she would be the most sociable person in the family, and the kindest, that she would be my social organiser, that she would have me dad-dancing in the kitchen on a Monday night. Nobody told me that she and I would be going to the football together every Saturday to watch her brother play.

Oh and did I mention the drama? She 'roped me in' to acting alongside her in a local drama group. Me! A typically grumpy middle-aged man who can now add 'amateur dramatics' to my CV, and I found out that I really enjoy it, nobody else on this planet could have done that!

Brian Murray, dad to Rachel

FAMILY DADS

When my wife and I first heard...

...the doctors' diagnosis that our daughter would most likely be born with Down syndrome, we didn't want to believe it. We kept saying to ourselves that it is impossible, it's not true, there must be a mistake, not us, not our daughter. We truly believed that everything was going to be OK ...and you know what? It was indeed.

Laura was born in July 2018. It was the most beautiful day in my life, in our lives. Long-awaited, our only, perfectly beautiful, beautifully perfect...our little girl. Yes, she was born with an extra chromosome, but it was completely irrelevant. The most important thing was that our daughter was with us.

Laura is now 18 months old. I can't imagine my life without her. She changed me, changed my wife, she changed our life ... for the better. Yes, sometimes it's not easy, sometimes it's hard work, there are bad days, there are moments of doubt, but seeing her growing every day, achieving the unachievable, making little steps, gaining new skills, nothing else matters!

She taught me to see and enjoy little things in my life, in our life; she taught me to live here and now, not tomorrow, not the day after, but today...

...and yes, you guessed it, she is daddy's little girl...she is the most beautiful gift God has given me in my life!

Chris Swiejkowski, dad to Laura

RODZINA OJCIEC

Kiedy po raz pierwszy usłyszeliśmy...

...„prognozę" lekarzy, że nasza córka najprawdopodobniej urodzi się z Zespołem Downa nie chcieliśmy wierzyć. Powtarzaliśmy sobie z żoną, że to niemożliwe, że to nie prawda, że się pomylili, że nie my, nie nasza córka. Do końca wierzyliśmy, że wszystko będzie dobrze...I wiecie co, było.

Laura urodziła się w lipcu 2018 roku. Był to najpiękniejszy dzień w moim życiu, w naszym życiu. Długo wyczekiwana, nasza jedyna, najpiękniejsza... idealna, nasza mała córeczka. Tak, przyszła na świat z bonusem -dodatkowym chromosomem, ale było to kompletnie bez znaczenia, najważniejsze, że była z nami.

Obecnie Laura ma osiemnaście miesięcy. Nie wyobrażam sobie życia bez niej. Nie wyobrażam sobie, że mogłoby jej z nami nie być. Ona zmieniła mnie, zmieniła moją żonę, zmieniła nasze życie... na lepsze. Owszem, czasem nie jest lekko, są gorsze dni, są chwile zwątpienia, jednak widząc jak każdego dnia rozwija się i małymi kroczkami zdobywa nowe umiejętności wszystko inne schodzi na drugi plan.

To ona nauczyła mnie zauważać małe rzeczy i cieszyć się nimi; to ona nauczyła mnie żyć tu i teraz, nie jutro, nie pojutrze, dzisiaj...i tak, Laura jest moją małą córusią tatusia. Jest najpiękniejszym darem jaki Bóg dał mi w życiu.

Mąż i ojciec - Krzysiek

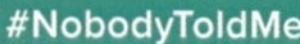

I sat and held Jaxon...

...I'd seen straight away he had Down syndrome. Why had no one said anything?

I handed him back to Lorraine, who was ecstatic. He settled down for a breast feed and I could see the relief on her face. He was here safe and sound.

I sat beside her and broached it gently.

"Do you think his eyes look a bit weird?"

"No", she replied, then she paused and said "do you think he's got Down syndrome?"

I nodded. She called in the midwives. It seemed as if half the medical professionals in the hospital came pouring in, six or seven midwives, paediatricians and doctors. Someone came and took blood from our tiny son.

They were all exclaiming how beautiful he was... My brain was shouting, "Shut up!! Stop saying he's beautiful! He's not beautiful, he's got Down syndrome!"

I was furious, devastated... Couldn't cope.

That feeling lasted a very short time as I quickly thought, "This is my son and Down syndrome isn't going to stop me loving him." He needed me to be strong and he was still the child we wanted.

Five years on he is cheeky, funny and the centre of our world. When I walk in from work I hear "Daddy!" and he races into my arms. He has made me a better person and I couldn't love him any more than I do.

Mark Buckmaster, dad to Jaxon

FAMILY

DADS

My son was always going to...

...be called Lennon from the moment I knew he coming into this world. I had a vision of the son of my dreams, a typical little boy. I imagined playing football, hide-and-seek, teasing Mummy, getting into general father-and-son mischief, and even looking forwards to our first beer together.

Lennon was born with Down syndrome and guess what? We play football, hide-and-seek, tease Mummy and get up to general father-and-son mischief. That first beer is only 13 years away.

I have a Beautiful Boy.

Paul Scutts, dad to Lennon

FAMILY DADS

When Jacob was born...

...the midwife said she thought he may have a chromosome-based condition. The consultant agreed and queried Down syndrome.

Three days it took to get the result. Three days spent saying, "they're all wrong" but deep down knowing they were right.

I wondered if I would ever feel the same for Jacob as I do for his older brother. Whether I would be excited on the drive home from work to see him. My thought process was very selfish, but it was mine to own.

I can say honestly that I know we still have obstacles to overcome, but little Jacob's smile is all I need to know we can do it. He is my world, and in the words of Stevie Ray Vaughan, he is my pride and joy.

Colin Vince, dad to Jacob

This is me and my son...

... Leighton who is now eight months old. Before Leighton was born my wife and I were told that Leighton might have Down syndrome. We refused testing to confirm as in our mind he was our son and nothing would change that. I doubted myself as a parent and whether I would bond with my son. I was also worried about what other people would think.

Leighton is an absolute joy and I love him more than words could ever say. He has the most incredible and infectious smile from the moment he wakes and every day I can't believe how lucky I am but also that I ever doubted our bond.

One hundred words just doesn't seem enough to describe my love for him. He has a very special bond with my wife Denise and our other son Brayden too.

John Martin, dad to Leighton

Nobody told me...

...that my son would become my biggest teacher.

He has taught me that there is no limit to what I would do for him.

Through the struggles we have faced he has shown that he would continue to fight on. Following his example we fought too and kicked the darkness until it bled purest daylight.

I've learned that even the smallest of gestures such as him holding my finger would centre me and unleash a torrent of love I never knew I had.

I've learned to smile at everything. Not only the good things but at the bad, his smile will melt away any ills. In his smile there is no truer happiness.

But my biggest lesson from Arthur would be this...

Love. No matter what.

Thom Axon, dad to Arthur

Ever since Dan was very young...

...I've taken him to our local football ground, Lydney Town AFC.

It's been a family tradition to follow them, long before he was born. I watched them play with my dad and grandad from the age of 10, and so it was nice to carry on the tradition with Dan. My dad still goes, so there's still three generations of Jones's cheering them on!

Dan loves going to the matches, he really looks forward to the games and over the years he's been team mascot in important cup games. They really do treat him like the 12th man, including him in team photoshoots, and even supplying him with team shirts with his name and number, always asking which number he would like on the back.

Mark Jones, dad to Dan

FAMILY DADS

Much like everyone else...

...we didn't know what sort of person our new child was going to be before Raquel was born. It was certainly a painful shock to find out, within a couple of hours of her being born, that Raquel most likely had Down syndrome.

Those early days were filled with questions and many emotions which I had not counted on experiencing as a new parent. We had an insight into the condition as Raquel's 12-year-old cousin also has the condition – but initially I could not fathom what the future held, despite the unquestioning adoration I had for our new arrival.

What are the expected health issues? Would she experience all the typical challenges associated with the condition? How different will this life be? How will our other child be affected? These were among the many thoughts I had – a lot.

The truth is that the answer to many of these questions are ongoing and will be answered bit by bit as time goes on.

Raquel will be 3 years old in a few months. She is a happy, adventurous and fascinating little girl who is progressing at her own pace. And so are we, as a family. I am happy with that and looking forward to the future.

Neil Donaldson, dad to Raquel

After having four boys...

...I figured it's bound to be another, so was delighted to discover we were expecting a girl, a beautiful little girl, my first ever girl, BUT she has Down syndrome. She isn't going to be normal, she isn't what I had planned and hoped for. What are people going to say? What sort of life could a person with Down syndrome have?

But how wrong was I? I can't believe how much I'm in love with her already and how strong she is.

If I could go back to the day we discovered Saffron has Down syndrome, I would say, You prat! Look how wrong you are, everything is going to be fine, and don't, whatever you do, don't search online, you won't like your findings.

Life with Saffron is better than I had ever imagined – the love and pride she has given this family is overwhelming and everyone is so in love with her.

Josh Wilson, dad to Saffron

FAMILY DADS

I was 41 when I found out...

...at long last I was going to be a Dad. The prenatal diagnosis of Down syndrome was a shock but our path was set and we eagerly awaited the arrival of our bundle of joy!

Teddy was born a healthy happy baby with no concerns and a confirmed diagnoses of mosaic Down syndrome and we happily celebrated.

But 18 months later, we received devastating news when I was diagnosed with Parkinson's disease, a degenerative condition that affects the brain and has many symptoms such as tremor, stiffness, slow movement, sleep issues, memory problems and depression.

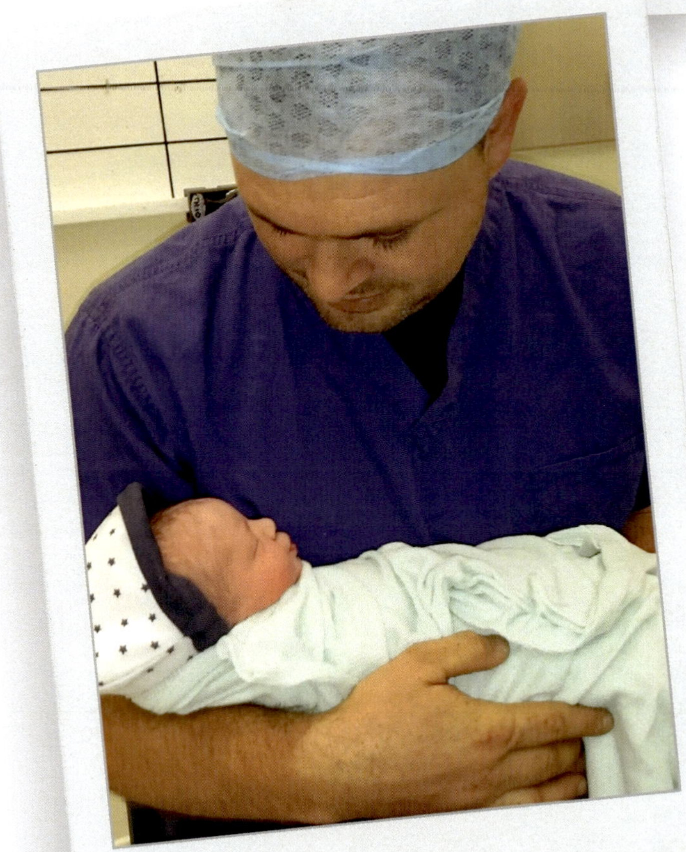

My condition gradually worsened and I struggled to cope with everyday tasks such as nappy changes, bathtimes and playtime. Chasing after an ever-growing Ted became more and more challenging, my fears for the future increased, and I didn't want to miss out on life with Ted.

Three weeks ago I underwent pioneering surgery, a four-hour operation where eight electrodes were implanted in two sections of my brain, and we cannot wait to start seeing the benefits and the promise of a full and continuing busy life with a now 5½-year-old Ted.

Andy Straight, dad to Ted

Nothing prepares you...

...for parenthood. Certainly, nothing prepares you for parenting a child with Down syndrome. Life has a way of taking sharp left-turns and when our second daughter, Chiara, was born, we were already on a sharp left-turn and thought this would take us to the edge.

It didn't.

My wife and I have varied careers: I'm a musician and travel up and down the country every week. She is the General Manager of the Flagship Ralph Lauren London Store and travels to New York, Milan, Tokyo and Paris. She also has Multiple Sclerosis.

We juggle. We manage. We live. We live fulfilling lives. A modern, slightly complicated family. There are extra doctor's appointments, classes, specialists and play dates. There are difficult moments but, mostly, there are belly-laughs and joy. Chiara has taught our whole family how to appreciate and revel in every goal achieved. We celebrate the tiny milestones that no one else sees. Every morning, Chiara chirps, "Wake up now!" She sets a great mood for the day. She is a blessing. We are proud of both our daughters, and thankful that we were lucky enough to have one with an extra chromosome.

Tim, dad to Chiara

FAMILY GRANDPARENTS

Nobody told me...

...how strong these babies are. I was fortunate enough to be with my son and daughter-in-law when Saffron was born and she arrived literally kicking and screaming. She really is a feisty little thing.

Nobody told me what a learning-curve I would find myself on. I have learnt so much over the last three months.

Nobody told me her love could heal old wounds.

Nobody told me I would fall head-over-heels in love the moment I looked into her perfect little face or that I would cry myself to sleep when she was struggling in the NICU.

And, finally, nobody told me the last three months would be among the best of my entire life.

Sarah Almond, grandmother to Saffron

FAMILY GRANDPARENTS

My gorgeous grandson Jake...

...was born five weeks early by emergency C-section in August 2018. Within 48 hours of Jake being in SCBU, my daughter was told that they wanted to test Jake for Trisomy 21. How was this possible when results during pregnancy had come back fine? Why wasn't it picked up during scans? Why didn't anyone prepare my daughter or us? My grandson was officially diagnosed with Down syndrome a week later.

As a parent and grandparent, it's a double worry. I had so many questions running through my head. Would my daughter reject Jake? Would my daughter cope with the challenges ahead? How would society react to my grandson? Would my gorgeous little grandson have disabilities? The list of questions was endless to say the least and the rollercoaster of emotions is indescribable but I needed to be strong even though inside I wanted to scream and cry. I knew that I loved my grandson regardless of any diagnosis and that I was prepared to support and proudly walk at my daughter's and grandson's side on their journey. All the same, it was a shock and this wasn't something I could fix; nor could I take away my daughter's pain and anxiety.

But my fears slowly vanished. My daughter is a great mother and adores Jake, and he is a happy one-year-old little boy.

My lovely grandson has the X Factor in more ways than one, not just because of the extra chromosome but because there is something so special and magical in the twinkle of his eyes, his beautiful smile and his adorable giggle. He can melt me in a nanosecond and he knows it. The past year has been an amazing rollercoaster and I would not change a single thing about him. He is perfect!

If I could go back to those first days, I would say to other grandparents, "Leave your worries aside and enjoy the moment because your grandchild will show you the way".

Eve Leli (nan) to Jake

FAMILY GRANDPARENTS

I would say to other grandparents...

...and parents who have just found out that their baby has or might have Down syndrome that, yes, some aspects of life will be different to what you think you were expecting but who knows what any life is about to bring?

My experience is this. Alice is a healthy, bright little girl who I love so much it hurts! Yes, I was upset when I knew she would have Down syndrome but the moment she was born the love was there and we all focused on how to help Alice reach her potential.

She has (among other things) physiotherapy, support from the Special Educational Needs team and Speech and Language Therapy plus amazing support form a local charity where Alice and her mum and dad meet other families who have children with Down syndrome. They learn from each other and support each other. Alice can sign (using Makaton) and at just over two and a half is now saying the first sound of many words. She is learning fast and communicates really well – using signs, by pointing and any other way she can. Speech is coming. She can stand up unaided and can walk well holding two hands and quite well holding one hand.

She has great empathy and picks up on our moods and feelings. She laughs so much and is very facially expressive. I look after her every Thursday and it is a day filled with joy and pride. Alice has an amazing family consisting of both sets of grandparents plus adoring aunties, uncles, cousins etc and masses of friends. Alice has travelled to very many countries with her family and is used to going on planes, trains and of course by car.

As you can see, I am a very proud nanny who is very hopeful for the future. However, I know we will come up against people who do not understand Down syndrome and we will no doubt have to fight for services. But I would not change our darling Alice for the world.

If you are the grandparent of someone with Down syndrome, you're the member of a very exclusive club and can gain entry to a wonderful closed Facebook page!

Jenny, nanny to Alice

FAMILY GRANDPARENTS

Beth told us she was pregnant...

...after having her 12-week scan in the UK and they said there were possibly problems. On the back of this we made the decision to bring her to live with us in Hong Kong and pay for her to be treated and give birth under private care. She had a scan at 20 weeks that was analysed by a much respected Hong Kong obstetrician who told us that Seth either had Edward's, Patau or Down syndrome and that Beth should seek a termination immediately.

We travelled home in silence. Whilst my wife and I are fanatically pro-life, we had to back away and let Beth make her own decision. It was fairly late when we got home and I poured myself a glass of wine and went and sat outside on the balcony. Beth came and joined me and we sat there for a few minutes in silence. Finally, I summoned up the courage to ask her, "What are we going to do?" She looked at me, stood on her feet and screamed, "I will not kill my child!" So I said, "Well that's that then", while crying fit to bust.

Following further tests the result came back as Down syndrome – Beth and I burst into tears and started laughing! The doctor looked at us and said, "Why are you laughing?" and Beth said, "It's only Down's!" She was advised to return to the UK immediately and get an abortion.

We made the decision that Beth would return to the UK to give birth there as Hong Kong is not remotely 'Down's friendly'.

Seth is turning four this year. He has spent three glorious, extended periods with us in Hong Kong. He has an incredibly supportive extended family, his cousins love him to bits, his mother loves him to bits but the funny thing is that when he is with us in Hong Kong, the Chinese think he is mixed race! The Filipinos call him blessed and his grandparents, privately, call him their favourite.

Trevor Butler, grandad to Seth

FAMILY GRANDPARENTS

Devon

On 4th May, my second granddaughter was born,
named Devon.
Before that day, we hadn't known that a special child was
On her way.
A heart defect was detected,
by the age of one, it had been corrected.

Devon came on in leaps and bounds,
Her smile charming everyone around.
We had our share of anguish
Due to seizures, pneumonia and sepsis.
Hospital appointments took up lots of time,
Her eyes, ears and her heart were fine.

Hypotonia caused her mobility to be slow
With a frame though, off she would go.
It was a joy to see Devon moving on her own
She grew stronger and soon she'd grown.

Devon only had a few words to say
But the songs she could sing would blow you away.
Devon, you've made my life so much richer
I'm so blessed to live close to you and your sisters.

In my lifetime I've seen a change of attitude
For which I am filled with gratitude.
Although some people still stare,
All they see is your Down syndrome and your
wheelchair.
They can't see the years that it's taken you
To achieve things that others can easily do.
How hard you've worked to sit up, crawl, and walk,
to eat solid food, communicate and talk.

Devon, you've brought me joy, sometimes pain,
Fear of losing you, but I'd do it all again.
Nanny couldn't be more proud of you,
I hope you know just how much I love you.

Ann, nanny to Devon

FAMILY GRANDPARENTS

I was in Spain at the start of a holiday

My daughter was pregnant and the due date was three weeks away. We were fitting in a quick holiday before we returned to be helpful grandparents and look after the other two little ones and admire the new addition to the family.

The phone rang. Ignacio sounded distant, distressed, unlike himself. Could we please come home? The baby was born, he had Down syndrome, and tears took over and he could no longer speak. He didn't need us to come home but he wanted us to, he explained through gulps of air.

We were all as a family in shock. We knew nothing about Down syndrome, feared the outcomes of such a birth. And then we met Luis. He was curled next to Anna in a private room at the hospital, calm, gentle. His sisters were devotedly gazing at him. Here was a new life, a cause for laughter and celebration. Why were we crying?

That seems like a lifetime ago, though it was only seven years. He shares books with glee, rushes into the sitting room to grab his favourites, pats the chair next to him to indicate exactly where you are to sit to read with him. He and his sisters, and his cousins up the road, have such fun together and Luis holds his own. In the park, at painting sessions, helping me with cooking, making houses in clay, cutting and sticking, and the beloved reading...we have such fun together. Hard to imagine that we cried. We now await his arrival for visits with excitement and look forward to his yell of "Bavra" and "Lollin", his names for his fond grandparents.

Avril Leigh, granny to Luis

FAMILY FRIENDS

For years and years...

...while working with adults with Down syndrome, people would say, "aren't (they) all loving and affectionate" and "always nice". Many of those who view Down syndrome from a distance assume that people with Down syndrome could in no way be individuals with their own individual, wants, needs, preferences and personality. How wrong so many people are!

This was highlighted when I met Claire, who has become a great friend. She's a confident, charismatic queen who knows what she wants and where she wants to be! She is an individual who shares the same emotions as you and me.

When Claire comes to events with me she steals the show – it is almost like she is a celebrity. This has nothing to do with her having Down syndrome but everything to do with her infectious character. She gets those party-poopers off their bums and onto the dance floor without fail! During these times I always look at her with so much pride, as she is one of those people who I know is changing the world.

I realise I heavily rely upon Claire for a large chunk of my happiness as her heart is pure and her character is huge! We all need somebody like Claire in our life, a friend that never sweats the small stuff and does not judge. She gives everybody a chance and if they let her down then it's their loss. But she never leaves anybody behind.

Amber McLeod, friends with Claire

FAMILY FRIENDS

Erin and Maddy...

...met a couple of years ago at their local Down syndrome support group. Each Saturday they meet up and enjoy keeping in touch by Facetime and messaging during the week.

Erin says of Maddy, “Maddy and I went to Strictly live. It was fun. Seeing her every week at Sports Club is just amazing.”

And Maddy of Erin, “Erin makes me laugh. We do fun things together, but sometimes we fall out.”

FAMILY FRIENDS

My best friend Stephanie

I first met Stephanie in Year 9 in high school. We were fresh-faced 13-year-olds with our whole lives ahead of us and the rest, as they say, is history.

I don't think of Stephanie as having Down Syndrome, because there's never been a reason to. She is independent, holds a good conversation, she has a good sense of humour and her outlook on life is inspiring. She cares about me, is reliable and trustworthy.

It has never bothered Stephanie that I wear glasses and that I can't see anything without them, or that my hair has changed length and colour since we met. She hasn't been fazed by the fact that I am shockingly bad at crazy golf or that sometimes I can never work out how to split the bill when our friends all go out for tea. Stephanie never treats me any differently and nor do I her.

Sometimes Steph can forget things (like what she did yesterday); so do I. Stephanie sometimes doesn't understand a joke; neither do I. At times, Stephanie can lose her bearings when we are out and about, and to be perfectly honest, my spatial awareness and geography skills are surprisingly poor for a 26-year-old! The message I am implying is that yes, Steph may struggle with certain life skills but, as it happens, so do I.

Throughout the past 13 years, Stephanie has become one of my best and closest friends. When we left school I became Stephanie's carer for 18 months. Within this time we attended fitness classes at our local leisure centre, we enjoyed weekly visits to a science centre, saw many films at the cinema and ventured out on various modes of transport. Not only did this time together strengthen our friendship, it strengthened our confidence, resilience

and responsibility. Since then, we have celebrated birthdays, played games of bowling and rounds of crazy golf, painted ceramic ornaments, been on walks, and – Stephanie's favourite – we have been to the beach!

Spending time with Stephanie is so refreshing. She is able to turn any situation into a positive and I thoroughly enjoy every second I spend with her. She has an infectious laugh, smile and personality and always seems so happy. She is so ambitious and brave and is willing to give anything a go. She loves to learn new skills, and with practice, she can do any activity. I have always found Steph to be considerate and mature when it comes to greeting and chatting to various people (ones she knows well and ones she has just met). She is thoughtful and has a good memory of events. She is friendly and capable.

I had never met anyone with Down syndrome before I met Stephanie. Since I have become her friend I have been welcomed into the vast Down syndrome community. I have been invited to parties and I have had the privilege of meeting her friends at other social events. Stephanie has a wonderful and enviable social life; from clubs to discos, parties to barbeques, she is never without an event to go to or look forward to. In these activities and gatherings she is surrounded by friends with other special needs and their families – a community in which she can flourish, grow in confidence and enjoy herself. Throughout the working week, Stephanie volunteers in a special-needs cafe where she has learnt how to make sandwiches and other meals on a menu. She now uses her experience to help new young adults who are just starting there, which is greeatly appreciated by the staff who run and support the café. Stephanie has used this invaluable experience of catering to work in other local cafes and has recently started a new job in a beauty salon.

She has also been a boon in her local community theatre group, where she is a part of their bi-annual performances, both acting and singing in the summer and Christmas productions. To be honest, I am surprised she can fit me into her extensive and exciting weekly routine!

I would like new parents of children with Down syndrome to know that your child is going to accomplish, achieve and have everything other children will. They are going to make you proud, happy, laugh and keep you on your toes. They are going to have friends and enjoy their lives, just like my friend Steph does.

Jenny Torrance, friends with Steph Nicholas

FRIENDS

I've grown up knowing Tom...

...and really enjoy spending time with him. Tom and I enjoy writing songs, watching sport and catching up on the latest "Strictly" episodes. Tom is an amazing friend as he never judges me or others and gives the best encouragement.

He's also got some good jokes.

My life is so much better with Tom in it, he brings out the best in me.

Connie, friends with Tom

FAMILY FRIENDS

James is a kind...

...and happy friend. I get on very well with James.

We are in the same classes and maths is our favourite lesson. We work together in lots of lessons and I sometimes help James with his spelling.

In Year 8 I had lots of fun with James and our friends and teachers in school making a video about how great it is to have James as a friend.

In the summer we like to go to Oakwood Theme Park. We both like the exciting rides. In the holidays we like to see each other. We both like Marvel films and swimming, James is a great swimmer. We have lots of fun together and laugh lots. This holiday we would like to meet up to go out for a meal.

I always like to be in James's company. I like everything about him and I think he will always be a best friend.

Joel, friends with James

Life goes on

The story now is that there is no story. The majority of families crack on with enjoying life. Their norm may be different to what they'd initially expected, but we all fall in step with our family's rhythm. Some of our children have more complex needs, often associated with having a dual diagnosis with autism – they too dance to their own tune.

LIFE GOES ON EVERYDAY LIVING

We have been lucky to have pupils...

...with Down syndrome at our primary school over the past five years. It has been a pleasure to contribute to the life journeys of these students, all of whom we believe will achieve every success in the future.

We feel we have been able to embrace the unique qualities that each of them possess and by ensuring their inclusion is completely successful, our school has been greatly enhanced. Whilst I find that children are natural celebrators of diversity and difference, I believe that our pupils with Down syndrome have supported the development of understanding within our wider community, removing the stigma that can sometimes be attached to pupils with additional needs.

Success at school for a pupil with Down syndrome is not always straightforward and it is an ever evolving challenge due to their unique learning profile. But when daily progress is made and inclusion is facilitated it makes you, your organisation, and your community stronger. The pleasure when you do get it right is phenomenal.

Mr Lowes, Inclusion Manager

LIFE GOES ON EVERYDAY LIVING

We have four children

The eldest, Isaac, is 15 and Kitty, the youngest who has Down syndrome, is 7 years old. Over the years we've faced many medical issues beyond everyday sniffles and bugs: hearing difficulties, temper tantrums, eyesight problems, enlarged tonsils, frequent chest infections, slow weight-gain, reluctance to eat, frequent tonsillitis, febrile convulsions, feeding difficulties, dyspraxia, small hole in the heart (which closed on its own), anxiety/phobias, visits to A&E, overnight stays in hospital...

...of this list, only one relates to Kitty alone (the heart one). The rest have been experienced by our "typical" children. Kitty has had some of these too but by no means all (or even most). The point is that all children bring with them complications and can certainly be a source of worry for us parents. But that doesn't take away from how amazing they are and how much we value and love them. It really is no different for children with Down syndrome.

Ursula and Crispin Adams, parents to Kitty

LIFE GOES ON EVERYDAY LIVING

We always felt that we were incredibly lucky...

...with Seb's primary school. They just "got it". He was included in everything, from school plays to residential trips, drama festivals and dance shows. I dreaded the day that he would have to leave but, as we know, time waits for no man and it was soon time to consider our next move.

We had no idea whether to push for mainstream or opt for our local special school. In my heart I wanted mainstream, as I like the idea of Seb growing up with people from his community that might see him out and about when he is an adult. We have already seen first hand how all of Seb's peers and friends see him as an equal. They know he needs support to achieve certain things but they don't see Down syndrome, they just see Seb. They celebrate his achievements and are always proud to have him in their groups or teams.

Choosing the right school was a major worry, but as soon as we walked into reception of the school that his primary feeds into, we felt welcome and the whole visit was really positive.

We are now in his third term. As before, it's gone way beyond my expectations. We have been blessed with some incredible professionals supporting Seb, caring parents and wonderful, thoughtful kids. Seb continues to be popular and has even made friends with children from a different primary school. He loves accessing so many different subjects: he particularly loves geography, science, food tech, drama and dance, he has a new-found interest in art and, of course, he loves playing rugby, football and basketball.

Academically, he is a long way behind his peers, but the school has been able to differentiate his curriculum and give him meaningful work – and as long as he is making progress then we view it as a success. The school disco was a standout moment for me this year. I went along to lurk in the shadows and make sure everything was OK. Seb, grasping every opportunity as always, marched straight onto the dance floor. He doesn't feel self-conscious at all and just naturally started dancing. He totally owned the floor and all the kids were chanting his name and joining in with him. I could never in my wildest dreams have imagined this day back when we were told our baby had Down syndrome.

One of the best things about having a child with Down syndrome is the incredible support network from within the community – something made all the more powerful in the age of social media. There are Facebook groups full of knowledge, expertise and experience; if you have a challenge or concern, or just something to celebrate, there are thousands of parents out there to help and/or celebrate with you. When Seb was a baby I feared the future. But I can honestly say, with each new milestone, I enjoy him more and all that he achieves. Nothing fills me with more joy than seeing Seb as he comes out of school, still smart and handsome in his uniform, checking his phone and saying goodbye to his friends – just like any other 12-year-old!

Caroline White, mum to Seb

BUNDESLIGA
LaLiga
Premier League
SURF CLUB

LIFE GOES ON EVERYDAY LIVING

Fourteen years ago my world...

...came crashing down around my ears, when five minutes after delivering our baby girl the midwife told my husband and I that she suspected Rachel had Down syndrome. My head filled with what I now know are outdated stereotypes of what Down syndrome was and what it would mean for our future as a family. None of this was helped by doctors who insisted on predicting what she wouldn't do and what sort of character she would have. "She might not walk or talk" and "she will be very passive", they confidently said.

Fast-forward to where we are now and I cannot begin to tell you how wrong those people were. Life is absolutely nothing like those predictions. Life with Rachel as part of our family is nothing less than utterly brilliant. Yes, we have had hard days; yes, when she was younger she had some horrendous operations (two lots of bowel surgery, one major eye operation) but what we have on a daily basis is a daughter who surpasses our expectations and is constantly surprising us with what she can do (the most recent being 24 quite complicated algebra equations completed correctly without any help). She has HUGE amounts of character. She is resilient, hard-working, witty, creative, single-minded, hilarious, active, chatty, extremely competitive, fashion-conscious and not in the slightest bit passive!

As for family life, I can honestly say that having Rachel hasn't stopped us doing anything. She needs a bit more help to do some things but she never, ever gives up and always gives things a go. She loves gymnastics, she does trampolining classes, goes to squash training at a local club with her brothers and climbed Snowdon at age 11. To be fair, that took a lot of bribery with Haribos but at the end of the day she made it all the way up (and down!) and she wasn't the only one in our group who needed to be fed sweets on the way. She has canoed down the River Esk, she has done gorge-walking and loves nothing more than going out on her tandem on family bike rides.

When she was born I worried about whether I would go back to work and my husband worried about the future. As it happens, I went back to work when Rachel was one year old and have worked pretty much ever since, although having Rachel has made me prioritise what's important to me and so I have had a big career-change. Rachel has had no negative impact on our family whatsoever. In fact, she has had a hugely positive impact on all of us and taught us patience, understanding, to celebrate the small things and I would never have imagined how proud I would be of her.

Rachel has two brothers – one 2 ½ years older and one 2 ½ years younger. I did worry about the impact on them of having a sister with a disability but, again, those worries were unfounded. They both love their sister fiercely, fight with her just as much as they fight with each other and have fun with her just as they do with each other. Both boys are growing up to be kind, considerate and understanding of difference: all positive attributes that I am not sure they would have developed to the same extent without having Rachel.

As for the future, well who knows? Those doctors in the early days didn't know and I certainly don't know exactly what's ahead for any of my family, never mind just Rachel. But what I do know is that Rachel will be just fine and I am sure she will achieve her dream, which she says is "living in my own house down the road so that I can have my friends round for parties." Nobody told us that when she was born!

Gillian Bowlas, mum to Rachel

EVERYDAY LIVING

Having a child with Down syndrome...

...should never stop you living life to the full.

This time last year were fulfilling a family dream, a six-week back-packing trip around Thailand. Me, my husband and our three young children, Elwood, (11), Billy (8) and Esmé (5).

We wanted to have some freedom of movement so we just booked our hotel in Bangkok and one week on Koh Phangan: that was pretty much it!

We spent a few days exploring Bangkok before heading slightly north for a few days, to the river Kwai and to visit an elephant sanctuary.

For me the elephant sanctuary was one of the top highlights: seeing the pure joy and excitement from Esmé when she saw her first elephant just wandering around was infectious to all around. The whole day was an absolute wonderment.

Deborah Byrne,mum to Esmé

LIFE GOES ON EVERYDAY LIVING

Our focus when Lucas was born...

...was first to get him through his heart repair, then think about his Down syndrome diagnosis. I guess our careers came a slow third for a few months, especially as we had two other children to think about.

However, life does get back to some kind of normality, and whilst there are definite and important compromises to be made, as a team we worked it out.

I was fortunate that my husband felt able to take charge at home whilst I continued my career and am now a managing director for a global business, aided, I am sure, by my greater understanding of talent in difference and a far wider experience of people from many backgrounds.

Lucas is now 13, happy and healthy and at mainstream school and my husband Phil works pretty much full-time running our local Down syndrome charity, and we feel like we have the right balance for us and our children.

Rachel Shatliff, mum to Lucas

LIFE GOES ON EVERYDAY LIVING

For the first couple of years...

...of Keira's life we were in receipt of benefits, which was a struggle. However, as it was just me and my daughter to focus on, we managed OK, and receiving extra financial support from her father helped (although he played a very limited part in Keira's life).

As Keira has got older she has had mobility issues, and Disability Living Allowance was for a while our breadwinner.

I now run my own business in events (hiring out entertainment equipment) and work from home as it best suits our lifestyle. I am a single mother and have to juggle everything alone, including attending Keira's appointments, housework, running a business, essential budgeting, doing activities etc.

We have no direct support network where we live but we manage. I am your average working-class mother who powers on with bringing up my daughter who is very happy and goes to a fantastic SEN school who have amazed me with Keira's all-round development in education.

Karen Holland, mum to Keira

LIFE GOES ON EVERYDAY LIVING

Hi, my name is George...

...and I'm 15. Apparently, I have Down syndrome and autism and my mum wants to let you know a little about us. Folk with Down syndrome can also be affected by autism, as of course can anybody in the population. If we have both Down syndrome and autism, we have a dual diagnosis, which makes life even more interesting and can present some extra challenges!

There has been a lot in the news and on social media about what children and young people with Down syndrome can get up to. It has been fab to get so many of us in the public eye and everyone looks really happy to be filmed and photographed! We've been seeing how much a person with Down syndrome can achieve and how much meaning their life has. Some get married, speak two or three languages, design clothes, model, paint, lecture, swim the Channel, work in cafes, act, dance – the list goes on and on. We want to be in this world and we enjoy our lives!

But what if you can't do any of those things? Is it OK? My mum wanted to say that life with me is pretty fab too and I am happy to be alive. I am different though – I am no talker – in fact one of my few words is "cuddle", but I say it a lot. I shout it out ecstatically when I hug and kiss the people I love. I also can't get dressed or use the bathroom alone, I always need lots of help, but we've got used to it now and it's just our version of normal. I am not that bothered that I am different because I have never known anything else and my sister loves me wildly just as I am. She says I'm a great brother 'cos I never take her stuff or annoy her! People who get to know me have even said that I have great charisma... whatever that means!

Mum says that it's good that kids with Down syndrome are in programmes and articles because it shows how much they can achieve, but she wants to remind everyone that's it's OK not to turn out like that too. I love life and I love my family and friends and they love me. We have fun and life is good. It's true that I am probably not a poster boy, but I am happy – and my family loves me just as I am because that's what families do. And, by the way, I can swim really well. I'm not sure what stroke it is that I use but it works for me!

Tatty Bowman, mum to George

LIFE GOES ON EVERYDAY LIVING

Nobody told me...

...that autism is nothing to fear, that it doesn't mean that your child will not make progress, will not love you or be sociable.

...that by confusing skill-acquisition with value we are all missing the point of what it is to be human.

...that any initial or additional diagnosis doesn't define your child.

...that by going on the journey with your child you will be transformed.

...that acceptance and then celebration is possible, if not inevitable.

...that autism brings its own beauty.

Lucy is 11 and has a dual diagnosis of Down syndrome and autism. She needs a great deal of support but when the support is right – when we understand her world and the way she understands it – she shines.

Debbie Austin, mum to Lucy

LIFE GOES ON EVERYDAY LIVING

When Kieran arrived...

...in our world with an unexpected little extra, I didn't know what life had in store for him or us. What I did know was that mostly love wins out and if I held him tight, loved him with all my heart and surrounded him with the support of our family, he would do alright.

And our boy has done more than alright. If I'd known then that 26 years I would later be standing in church hearing him say his vows to the woman he loves, I wouldn't have worried for one moment.

Life isn't always easy, it's full of challenges but let's not forget it's also full of amazing joys.

My advice is to keep the faith, talk to anyone who'll listen in your worried moments and fill the fridge with tonic to go with the gin you'll be drinking!!!

Tessa Duffy, mum to Kieran

LIFE GOES ON EVERYDAY LIVING

***"This wedding day was extraordinary for many reasons. But possibly one of my favorite moments was the special first look Ashley planned for her little brother, Nick"*, writes photographer Kelsey, who beautifully captured that special time bride Ashley shared with her brother Nick.**

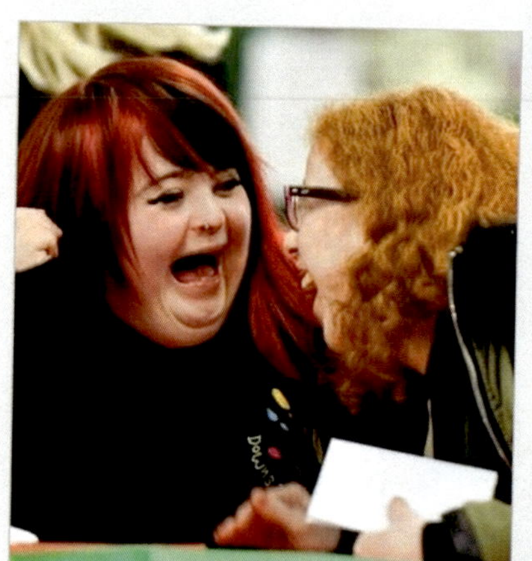

OF BELONG
Est. 2015

STAR WARS

VANS

#MoreAlikeThanDifferent

LIFE GOES ON ASPIRATIONS

Rebecca wants to perform on stage, preferably in High School Musical.

Jessica is an aspiring pop star, a singer/songwriter extraordinaire.

Charlotte wants to star in Eastenders and work for the police.

Ben wants to have a girlfriend, live in his own house, drive a car and be a postman or an actor.

Hollie has always said she wants to be a vet dentist.

Jack wants to play football for Nottingham Forest or Man U, and drive a fast sports car.

Holly wants to be a dancer with Katy Perry or Pink.

Ellie wants to be a hairdresser and make people happy.

LIFE GOES ON ASPIRATIONS

Jake loves cooking and wants to have his own restaurant.

James would like to live in a house with his wife and a dog and would like to work in the police.

Shelby wants to be a hair dresser, get a house and a dog and make gluten-free treats for everyone.

Samantha would like to be a makeup artist.

Jessica wants to be a nurse, go on holiday with Olly Murs and marry her boyfriend Joe.

Matt would like to work on the turnstiles at Notts Forest and have lots of pretty blonde girlfriends.

Riley wants to be a gymnast and to learn to drive a car.

Morgan would like to work in catering.

LIFE GOES ON ASPIRATIONS

Maya wants to be a triple threat (singer, actor, dancer) and a judge on Strictly.

Isaac would like to be a rockstar when he grows up.

Leila would like to work in Curry's. She is a washing-machine enthusiast.

Elise wants to be a police officer or a cook to make gluten-free food. She just wants to help people.

Eleanor wants to work with animals and is doing a course that includes animal care and dog grooming.

Miles would like to be a policeman when he grows up; failing that he would settle on being an astronaut.

Rachel wants to be a waitress AND a make up artist, and to live in her own house.

Joe wants to be a rock star but will settle for chief of police or working at McDonald's.

LIFE GOES ON ASPIRATIONS

Ben would like to play the villain in a pantomime, live in his own flat, and work in an Italian restaurant.

Jess would like to be a singer, dancer, cook, makeup artist or Youtuber... so long as she is in the limelight.

Poppy wants to do hair and beauty, work in Tesco and get a flat so mum and dad can sleep over.

Callum would like to work in a hotel or be rap star! And to move into his own flat with his girlfriend.

Lucas wants to be a parent, a great husband and to work at Tesco like his brother.

Tom wants to work in a school, have a flat, a wife and a dog and to ride a motorbike.

Matthew wants to work in Waitrose, not Tesco or Morrisons as uniforms are the wrong colour.

Jake wants to be a hairdresser or a teacher and he can't wait to get married.

LIFE GOES ON LIVING THE DREAM

I was 26 back in 2010...

...and at that time I was working on my first full-time job with Mencap Cymru in Cardiff as the Project Officer for a citizenship project with schools and colleges throughout Wales called "Partners in Politics". I have been lucky enough to have been able to "have my voice heard" in other important places too including at the House of Commons, the European Parliament in Brussels and, perhaps the most exciting of all, speaking at the United Nations Headquarters in New York. More opportunities came for me during the past five years as the self-advocate Council member for Europe for Inclusion International, taking me to many places around the world to meet other self-advocates.

The past decade also saw me be elected as a Community Councillor for my local area nine years ago, a role I still hold, carrying the Olympic Torch in Cardiff before the 2012 Olympics and, perhaps most important of all, meeting my boyfriend, Simon, 8 years ago.

In October 2019 I was very honoured to be nominated to attend the "Women of the Year" lunch and awards ceremony at the Royal Lancaster Hotel in London to celebrate my work and that of 400 other women from across the country.

It was a fantastic experience and a day I will never forget. As soon as we arrived at the hotel we spotted the red carpet and the paparazzi and almost immediately along came one of the judges, TV star Lorraine Kelly, who welcomed me. During the day I had the opportunity to meet lots of other guests including Mel Giedroyc, Dame Tanni Grey-Thompson, Angela Rippon, former Prime Minister Theresa May, Maureen Lipman, Zoe Wannamaker and my favourite character from "Eastenders", Tamzin Outhwaite, who played Mel Owen until she got killed off! After a wonderful lunch came the Awards ceremony during which we heard some very personal and moving stories from some truly inspirational women, which reduced us all to tears! Perhaps the most emotive story was that of the Bletchley Park Ladies, who played such a big part in the war effort for our country and made a huge impact on the room when they took to the stage.

I have worked for Mencap Cymru, the leading organisation supporting people with a learning disability in Wales, for 13 years and worked on a number of projects. I am currently the Project Officer on the "Play Our Way" project, funded by Children in Need, which brings young people, both with and without a learning disability, together through inclusive sport and other activities. The project helps young people increase their confidence, improve their teamwork and build meaningful friendships to help change attitudes towards learning disability for the next generation and break the stigma felt by some people. From March 2020 I am starting a new role with Mencap Cymru as External Affairs Officer, which I am very excited about. I am also an elected member of Mencap's Our Voices council, a board made up of representatives from across the country who have a learning disability and meet monthly in London to help advise Mencap on its priorities and decisions.

And so to the future!!!! Who knows what it will bring? What I DO know is that one day I will be living more independently, even though I am very happy living at home at present.

Outside my work I enjoy dancing, music, and especially drama, and I have been a member of Hijinx Theatre Company for the past 11 years. This has given me the opportunity to go on two professional national tours, and participate in many performances at the Wales Millennium Centre in Cardiff Bay, where we are based. I love spending time enjoying live music with my boyfriend Simon.

I do feel passionate about promoting equality in all I do. At a recent Inclusion Europe conference I attended in Graz in Austria, a new phrase emerged, which I think is very powerful. It was, “If you dare to speak up, inclusion happens”. Together with my own motto ‘Down syndrome....so what!’ I live my life believing that anything is possible.

I do hope that the coming decade will provide me with many more wonderful experiences like those I have enjoyed over the past ten years and that I can continue to try my best to make a difference.

Sara Pickard

LIFE GOES ON LIVING THE DREAM

I'm Bethany and I enjoy the cinema, swimming, bowling, singing and dancing. I live with my two sisters, mom, dad and pets I have two dogs, one called Monty and the other called Belle. I work at West Mercia Police Station in Worcester two days a week where I focus on administration. I sort out the post and organise the stock including pencils, rulers etc. I'm doing a level 2 diploma course in administration and have applied to do level 3 next year. I've had a total of 40 driving lessons and I'm looking into taking my theory test very soon.

I'm Hayley and I'm 23 years old and from Harlow in Essex. My favourite thing to do is acting and singing. I belong to two drama groups and have performed at the 02 Centre and the London Palladium. I work four days a week in a tea rooms which is run by others like myself. We always get fully booked as the customers get great food and always have a sing-along. I often go horse-riding with my cousins. I love going to the cinema and to parties.

LIFE GOES ON LIVING THE DREAM

I am James and I am 26. I live in Weymouth with my parents but after Heidi and I get married we will live in her flat in Coventry. At home I enjoy carpentry, computers, social media and arts and crafts. I am learning to do the housework, shopping and cooking. I enjoy going to Dorset Abilities group, a group for people with learning difficulties to help with writing skills, budgeting skills and money skills. I do "tuck by truck" where we take tuck to offices and factories. I help sorting out the money for it. We also do activities like sports, bowling and cinema trips.

I am Heidi and I am 24. When I was 20 I moved into my own flat with support staff for 22.5 hours a week. I work in a kids hair salon. I take the payments, do the social media and the stock-taking, sweep the floor and amuse the children. We are very excited to be getting married in July. James and I both have Down syndrome, but this does not hold us back from doing anything! We have fun and fulfilled lives!

LIFE GOES ON LIVING THE DREAM

I'm Emily. My week is amazing. I do swimming and gym, cinema and shopping, coffee and eating out. I've got Lily my PA – we do aqua-fit and jump-fit and girly sleepovers and movie nights in and make food for tea. I do photography and I go to the studio to do my creative writing and make films for my work. I work at The Cutting Room – it's all about my money for my employment and I do my jobs well. I spend my wages on Costa coffee, magazines and new clothes. I go to church every Sunday. I volunteer in the coffee shop there. I would love to do a midnight glow-in-the-dark walk with flashing lights to raise money for children at the hospice because I have a caring heart. I'm living my best life.

I'm Connor. I am 25 years old and live in Colorado where I enjoy hiking, swimming, cycling, martial arts, video games, acting and public speaking. I have earned my black belt in taekwondo and an Emmy. My award-winning film acting projects have been shown around the world. I would like to visit London, Thailand and Hawaii. I love pasta, cheese and mangos and would like to study cooking in New York.

LIFE GOES ON LIVING THE DREAM

Hi, my name is Alice, I am 21 years old and I live in Dorset with my mum and dad. I am an auntie to two nephews. I loved being a bridesmaid for both of my sisters. I go to college where I study Catering & Hospitality and work in the café. My hobbies are swimming, drumming, singing, acting and dancing. I go to an amazing theatre company every week on a Thursday evening. I sometimes have a sleepover at my best friend Grace's house. We've been friends for ten years since starting high school (when I used to live in West Sussex). In my future I want to move out to my own flat and work as a chef.

My name is Fionn and I live in Galway. Through good support, I have my own apartment, co-direct a social enterprise, and travel the world. We have filmed 600 interviews, including many celebrities, asking people what they love. With over 300,000 views online, I'm a bit of a celebrity myself. I love playing my fiddle, reading books, and making art with my dad. I've exhibited work in four countries. I teach children about wildlife for the Heritage Council, and guest lecture in Social Care at universities in Ireland and beyond. I advocate for others by treating my life like research. We call it The Happiness Project.

LIFE GOES ON LIVING THE DREAM

My name is Tom and I am 23 years old. I live in my own flat with support for travelling into London for work. I do my own cooking and look after myself. I have two paid jobs as a barman and a catering assistant. I am a powerlifter and I just did a competition where I won best junior lifter. I will be doing the British championships next. I like supporting my football team, I go to lots of matches. I like going to Youth Club and seeing my friends. I really want to live in my house with a friend one day.

I am Rachel. I am 19, I live in Edinburgh and I have three brothers and sisters. I love to chat and laugh with people. I have been learning to cook at college. I like to watch football and to dance. Dad and I act in a drama group together. My dream is to own my own business and get my own flat near my family and friends.

LIFE GOES ON LIVING THE DREAM

I am a landscape and wildlife photographer. My photographs are important to me. They're my life. I see pictures day in, day out. They matter to me. I want my pictures in more books and magazines. I want to travel to different places in the world and take pictures everywhere. My pictures tell a story. That's what I think. This is me, my world, my view, and I have inspiration for doing it. With my photography, it's all about the feeling. If it's a landscape or a bird or animal, it still catches me in that moment. My job is to be out there taking pictures.

Oliver Hellowell

I'm Bethany. I've always dreamed of being an actress but never thought it would actually happen. I was lucky enough to visit the set of my favourite programme, The Dumping Ground, in 2016 and it was then that I told my mum I wanted to act. A few years later I was asked to audition for the show and I was cast in the part of Ivy. I couldn't believe it. Dreams really do come true! I have been lucky enough to act with some excellent actors such as Rob Lowe and I recently worked with Lee Ryan from Blue and he was really kind and believes in me.

LIFE GOES ON LIVING THE DREAM

Kieran and Emmie were married in August 2019 and had a wonderful day celebrating with friends and family. Emmie wants to be Kieran's wife for ever and Kieran wants to be a good husband, have a nice home and cuddle his best girl everyday! Keep living the dream, guys!

Hi! My name is Kathleen Humberstone. I'm 21 years old. I live with my family in Surrey. I am a model. I've done modelling for two years, especially with River Island. I was born in Saudi Arabia. My parents lived there. And then we moved to Dubai, then India and then China. Finally, we moved to the UK. I am bilingual English-French because my mum is French. I have a boyfriend called Jack, he is also 21 like me. We've been together for nine years. I gave a speech at the United Nations in Geneva when I was 17, about my life with Down syndrome. I like to exercise every day to be healthy. Last year, I completed the Thames Path Challenge, 25km in nine hours non-stop. It was very tough but also incredible because I got my medal!! I was also very happy to be included in *Elle* magazine's 50 Game-Changers List of 2019. I walked at the London Fashion Week last September and I wore three outfits! I love my life!!

LIFE GOES ON LIVING THE DREAM

Hello, my name is Francesca. I am 18 years old and I have Down syndrome. I have an older sister called Cecily and we live with mum and dad. In primary and secondary school, I made friends and having Down syndrome didn't stop me joining in activities other than hockey. I achieved three GCSEs in IT, Food Tech and Combined Science. I got my Bronze DOFE in secondary school. I am now at College on a Foundation course and I am currently doing my Silver DOFE. Dancing is my passion. I love being with my friends, I love the music and I enjoy learning routines. In March 2019, I was invited to the UN in Geneva, along with others, to speak about work experience. I was very nervous but I was happy in the end.

Hello, I am Nino Genua. I am 21-year-old young man who goes to college. I am a model with Zebedee Management. I am a Community Coach, a Special Olympic Swimmer and the goalkeeper for a local team in Bristol. I support Bristol City, and manager Lee Johnson is my great friend. I go to the training ground with their first team. My girlfriend is Olivia. We have been together for five years, she is beautiful and perfect. Sport is my future and very important to me. I love my family, girlfriend and friends, and I love my life.

Before I discovered the page I was terrified and felt so alone. Discovering PADS has been a lifeline.

Having a safe space to go where you can vent your frustrations but also celebrate your achievements and have people right there with you every step of the way, is invaluable.

We were really struggling getting our heads around our baby having Down syndrome. Everyone has really helped us to see what life is like and to not be afraid but enjoy.

I have made friends, life long friends. Friends that can help with the smallest and toughest questions. It's a blessing to know we are not alone.

PADS has been a lifeline for us and a lot of families like us.

No matter what time of the day or night it is, it's always really handy to know you can just log onto Facebook and hopefully find someone to help with whatever problem you have.

The support, advice and encouragement we've received has been amazing, we wouldn't manage without it.

It makes your heart full of joy seeing everybody, it gives us hope and shares the love, happiness and the worry. It's such a lovely feel good page.

We have had so much reassurance and guidance from the page.

It's been amazing from the second we joined to ask advice from other parents, to make friends, to get to know other people and to see all the other beautiful babies.

Being able to share our journey with people that are on the same path and sharing the good and the bad days has made such a difference.

I found a community of support and I no longer felt alone. Thank you for empowering others near and far to embrace this amazing journey that we are on.

Before I joined the group I felt alone but once I joined I found what now feels like an extended family.

I didn't want to join this group, I didn't want to hear everyone pretending everything's gonna be fine. But actually people are just honest, when I'm having a crap day I say so and no one judges, people care and they've helped me so much.

Seeing other parents on the same life journey as us and seeing them in the same situation was something that gave me hope for his future.

The PADS Facebook group for expectant mums has been invaluable - it has immersed me in a world with loads of people who have been in my position or are in my position. Totally non-judgemental, everyone just wanting to offer advice, information, or a virtual hug.

The group has helped me in countless ways. I joined the evening of my diagnosis and instantly I felt like a weight had been lifted and someone had switched the light on again. I can't thank the ladies enough for all their advice and virtual hugs.

I love seeing how well everyone's kids are doing – such a happy positive place.

Nobody gets it unless you're actually in the same situation... so it's been amazing to be able to meet and chat with other mums who have the same concerns and worries, and to be able to see and hear from those further down the line- to see that everything's going to be ok.

This is the only Facebook page my partner will go on – he hates social media but even he says this is a lifeline!

For pregnant women living in the UK who are expecting a baby with a high chance/confirmed result of having Down syndrome.

https://www.facebook.com/groups/415274562687672/

Exclusively for new parents of a little one (aged up to 12 months) with Down syndrome and based in the UK.

https://www.facebook.com/groups/2188980851370457/

This book is designed to provide information and motivation to our readers. The content of each story is the sole expression and opinion of its author(s), and not necessarily that of the editor or the publisher. No warranties or guarantees are expressed or implied by the publisher's choice to include any of the content in this volume. Neither the publisher nor the individual author(s) shall be liable for any physical, psychological, emotional, financial, or commercial damages, including, but not limited to, special, incidental, consequential or other damages.

The book has been created by a mum who wants to show the world that there's nothing to fear about having Down syndrome. If I have inadvertently missed an image or a credit, misspelt a name or incorrectly quoted someone, my apologies. I hope our honest experiences show the reader why we're so proud of our children and young people and are Positive about Down syndrome.

PHOTO CREDITS:

Agata Sroka (12, 13); Andrei Kertesz (front cover, 119, 140); Barefoot Photography (33); Capture a dream (116); Clare Keylock (front cover); Dan Clarke (73); Daniela D'Amato (5); David White (123); Dinky Days Photography (43); Flash Bang Photography (26); Gillian Clarkson (123); Hello Gorgeous Studios (70); Ian Rice (141); Joy Sullivan (19); Kelsey Gene (120, 121); Leah Lloyd (17); Lisa Grace (2); Lucy Rae (7); Michael McGuire (66); Murat Ozkasim (140); Neal St Productions BBC1 (46); Nicole Perkins (56, 141); Oak & Claw Photography (29); Robyn Lee (57); Sadie Osborne (137); Sarah Cockerton (7); Sitting Pretty Photography (7); Sue Smalley (58)

Huge thanks to copy editors
Aviva Leeman and Susie May

with thanks to DSUO for their support!

If you would like to support PADS, any donation will ensure we can provide information and support to more prospective, expectant and new parents, and to provide training to medical professionals.

https://uk.virginmoneygiving.com/charities/downsyndromeuk